THE FLOW OF PURPOSE

Design and deliver

a better business

through shared purpose

By Keith Shering

The Flow of Purpose

The right of Keith Shering to be identified as the Author of the Work has been asserted by him in accordance with the Copyright, Designs and Patents Act 1988.

All rights reserved. Apart from any use permitted under UK copyright law no part of this publication may be reproduced , stored in a retrieval system, or transmitted in any form or by any means without the prior written permission of the publisher, nor be otherwise circulated in any form of binding or cover other than that in which it is published and without a similar condition being imposed on the subsequent purchaser.

Product or brand names used in this book may be trade names or trademarks. Where believed to be the case, the name has been used with an initial capital, or capitalised in the style used by the name owner. Regardless of capitalisation, brand names have been used in an editorial manner, rather than implying any endorsement or affiliation.

This publication is sold with the understanding that neither author nor publisher is engaged in rendering legal, accounting or other professional services. If legal or expert advice is needed, the services of a competent professional should be sought.

© Keith Shering 2018

ISBN-13: 978-1728761916

The Flow of Purpose

To all those who have taught (and still teach) me about what Purpose really is and why it matters.

Contents

Introduction 5
1   Why Does This Book Exist? 7
Part One – The Philosophies 13
2   What Is Purpose and How Can It Flow? 15
3   What Is A Business? 18
4   People And Purpose 27
Part Two – The Preparation 31
5   Why Take Time To Prepare? 33
6   Exploring The Organisation 36
7   Exploring Purpose 44
8   Exploring Selling 54
9   Exploring Propositions 59
10   Exploring Profit 69
Part Three – The Practicalities 75
11   The Flow of Purpose – Making It Happen 77
12   Set Your Purpose & Strategy 78
13   Let Your Purpose Flow 94
14   The Tools 99
15   Share Priorities 103
16   Find Stakeholders 125
17   Explore Processes 137
18   Purposeful Planning 161
A Call To Action 179
19   Start Your Flow of Purpose 180

Introduction

Introduction

The Philosophies

The Preparation

The Practicalities

Share Priorities

Find Stakeholders

Explore Processes

Purposeful Planning

Introduction

1 Why Does This Book Exist?

Most of us want to make our businesses work better. Be more profitable. A better place to work. More rewarding for customers. More resilient.

But why does it often seem so difficult, especially when we need to get other people to join us in that journey?

It can feel exhausting – trying to get others to join you in making changes happen.

I've been there many times. I've spent nearly 25 years working with businesses and on projects; as an analyst, consultant and manager.

I began to realise that the projects and changes that went well were those where everyone "believed". They were led by people who painted an honest yet compelling vision of what was needed. They made everyone feel like they could and needed to contribute.

People at all levels knew there was a bigger picture that bound them together. They shared a compelling purpose.

I'd spent time reading about the power of "why" and positively influencing people with "because". This fitted well with the idea of creating shared purpose across teams.

Introduction

I decided to re-examine the approaches that I used to analyse businesses and create strategy and vision. I set out to see how I could drive "purpose" (the "why") through the methods (the "what and how") to reach and connect people. I wanted to connect the stages along the vision, analysis and change journey using shared purpose.

I wrote The Flow of Purpose to collect together some of these experiences and share the learnings from my work. I hope it will stimulate thoughts, generate ideas and help you move your business or organisation forward.

I enjoy the learning that I get from every project I work on. As I help people to explore their business, so I discover more about how to improve The Flow of Purpose tools and approach. If you have feedback or suggestions as you read the book, or use the tools, I'd love to hear from you: **hello@theflowofpurpose.com**

What is The Flow of Purpose?

The Flow of Purpose is the way we make every business action meaningful to people, by linking it with a core, driving purpose that crosses over job or departmental boundaries.

With a flow of purpose, everything we do in our business has meaning. To us, to the people later in the process, to the people who passed the task on to us, to our colleagues and to our customers.

Everyone is playing a part in something that matters. We're all making changes and improvements that matter. The Flow of Purpose is about finding that purpose, that meaning, getting it as clear as it can be, and getting people to buy in to it.

Introduction

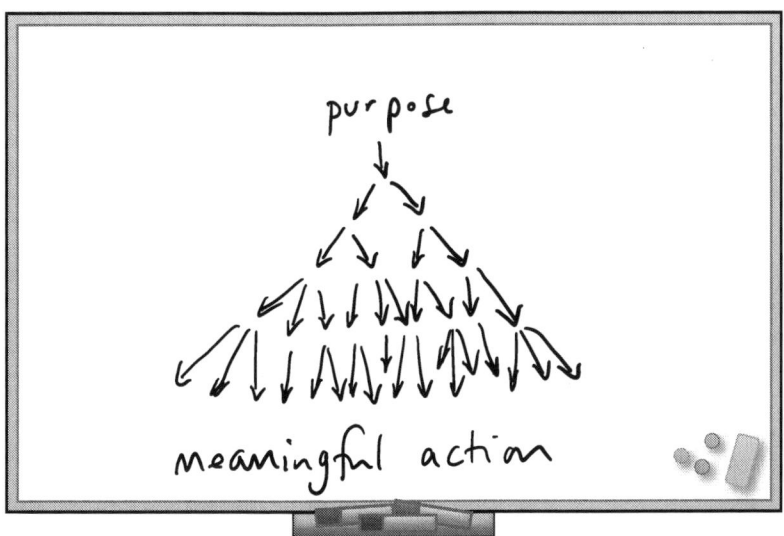

Figure 1 The Flow of Purpose brings meaning to everyone's actions

The Flow of Purpose shares the collection of philosophies and some of the tools I've built up over the years. These are simple yet effective things I've settled on to help my clients analyse and improve their businesses. Ideally, not as lone individuals, but as teams of people committed to positive change. Committed to work together because shared purpose runs through the philosophies and tools.

The philosophies and approaches I'll take you through are a result of many things. Experimentation, trial-and-error, design thinking, contemplation, and most importantly, reading, doing, listening and learning. They are ways of pulling people together around not just the "what and how" of solving problems, but the clear and compelling "why" – The Flow of Purpose through change and through business.

When do you know you have a flow of purpose through your organisation? When you ask people in any role "why do we do things this way?" and you get the same compelling answer from everyone.

Who Can Use The Flow of Purpose?

This is a book for leaders, whether formal or not; and for business owners and managers. It's perfect to use it "top down" starting with the CEO; but it can also help you change your own department or team and deliver better operation and results, whatever your level.

The Flow of Purpose works best in businesses and organisations with teams of staff, but it can be used for individuals and micro businesses too. Sometimes it's useful to remind yourself of your personal "big why", especially when trying to juggle the many demands of running a business.

The techniques in this book are primarily aimed at organisations that are "information-rich" - i.e. you create, pass on and share information, data or knowledge to make your decisions, provide your service, or do your work. That said, information and collaboration are so pervasive nowadays, that there are very few organisations that wouldn't benefit from using purpose to drive improvement.

Philosophy, Prep and Practicalities

My personal mission is all about maximising potential. I love to help people and businesses be the best they can be, through analysing their situation, setting vision, creating ideas, and taking action to make changes. Wanting to share with people how I aim to help with this is what led me to write The Flow of Purpose.

In The Flow of Purpose I'll take you through:

- the philosophies I've learned so far
- what they mean for looking at your business, and lastly
- the simple, accessible tools I use to analyse businesses and deliver change.

The Flow of Purpose is first about philosophies. These are the reasons why we might or might not do things or behave in certain ways. I've had the great fortune to work with some amazing businesses and leaders over the years. Every project I work on teaches me something about how to (or how not to) achieve something and vitally, *why* these approaches work (or not). I've attempted to pull together much of what I've learned into The Flow of Purpose, to share the wisdom of these leaders and visionaries.

The Flow of Purpose is also a resource for people wanting to analyse and probe their business processes and operations.

Introduction

Part Two of the book shares many of the key questions I've learned to ask to learn about clients' purposes and organisations. These can act as great jumping-off points for your own questions. (They can also show others that you're not the only one that asks awkward questions that are difficult to answer...). Part Two is a reference that you can read to prepare yourself to use The Flow of Purpose. It's also handy to refer back to as you use the tools, for some inspiration on questions to ask. Add your own notes and ideas in the margins as you go – make it your resource too.

The third part of The Flow of Purpose is "the instruction manual" itself. It's the walkthrough of the tools I've settled on as being the leanest, simplest, friendliest ways of turning purpose into results. You can leap ahead and get stuck in to Part Three if you wish; but it makes most sense when you've thought of your own philosophies and done your own preparation. I hope you'll find time spent with the first two parts of The Flow of Purpose is worthwhile and thought provoking. They are where you make this book your own.

Now, it is time to design and deliver a better business, built on purpose.

Introduction

Part One – The Philosophies

Introduction

The Philosophies

The Preparation

The Practicalities

Share Priorities

Find Stakeholders

Explore Processes

Purposeful Planning

Part One – The Philosophies

2 What Is Purpose and How Can It Flow?

A huge amount has been written about purpose, by cleverer people than me. But since we're talking about purpose, I should define what I understand it to mean. My handy Collins English Dictionary tells me:

Purpose n. reason for which something is done or exists; determination; practical advantage or use.

Taking this definition, I see The Flow of Purpose as:

The wilful and coordinated sharing of reasons and determination to do things that create advantage.

It's not a scattering, it's a flow. We must make purpose follow channels that are clear and understood. We need to work on defining channels and keeping them clear. Channels are things like communication, delegation, escalation and accountability (maybe using RACI matrices).

Part One – The Philosophies

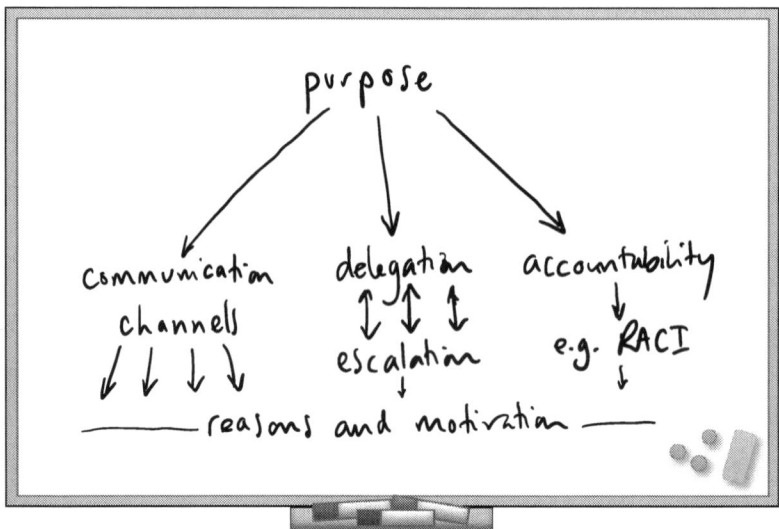

Figure 2 Flow needs channels

The reasons for doing our things – work, tasks, making decisions – should be clear, and we should make clear the reasons why we in turn need things done. We should be willing to stand up and discuss reasons and their validity. If we can't answer challenges as you use the tools o our reasoning convincingly, do we have truly valid reasons or a true purpose?

There should be overall advantage as a result of The Flow of Purpose and determination. Sometimes The Flow of Purpose makes our job easier, because people are aligning their determination with our need. They do something extra that helps us do better work overall. Other times we need to understand that we must shoulder some extra burden for the greater purpose.

Part One – The Philosophies

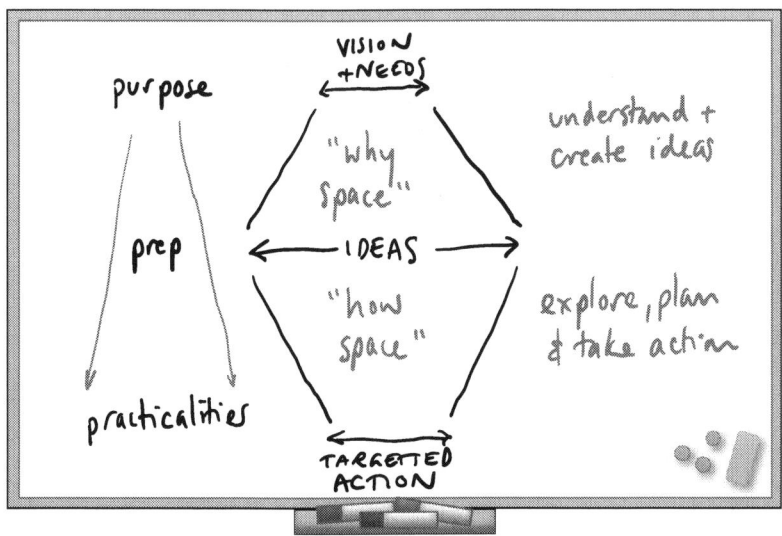

Figure 3 The Flow of Purpose can change how roles work

Purpose can only flow if we believe that it exists (or should exist) everywhere in our organisation. We need to help people understand why purpose matters, and how it can make a difference. Flow turns purpose into ideas that drive meaningful action.

Having a clear sense of how Purpose flows can help people re-invent their own roles. Thinking of "new whys" can lead to radically new "hows" through visionary ideas that give targeted action and improvements.

If I may get a bit prosaic, we need to share clear purpose to avoid the pools of cynicism that sink and swallow the promise of good ideas. Scepticism is fine – it asks for explanations and seeks belief, but cynicism is a real killer of purpose.

Let's start by looking at what a business (or other organisation) actually does…

Part One – The Philosophies

3 What Is A Business?

The bedrock of The Flow of Purpose is understanding how the elements of our business (or organisation) fit together, and how purpose relates to each.

Let's start by considering your business, its meaning and some of the questions and thinking points I've discovered over the years.

A note: I'll talk about "business" in this chapter, but the philosophies apply to charities and public sector too; with a little change of emphasis or wording – I'll share some of these as we go…

My definition of a business is:

An organisation with purpose that sells products or services to make a profit.

That sounds so simple as to be almost useless; "Yeah, thanks for that, Keith…"

But let's look at it a bit more deeply, bit by bit.

An Organisation…

An organisation is built by organising people. Their skills. Their time. Their attitude, culture, personalities. Their leadership and commitment. Their motivation and their desires. Their willingness to follow and their willingness to challenge.

Or their lack of any of these on any given day (especially after long weekends or cup finals)…

All these people things need to be structured (to at least some degree) for tasks to be done, processes to run and customers to be served.

But how many of these things are static, predictable and easy to structure and organise? Hmm, I can probably guess the answer to that one…

So, to help us cope with the frailties, variability and endless possibilities of people, we write processes to guide us & build systems to govern us.

We constrain people. Perhaps "channel them" is a kinder way of putting it. Nonetheless, following someone else's process, from some distant historical period, using a system no-one believes in, asks a lot of the people in an organisation. Do they believe in our processes & systems?

Generally speaking an individual is in a role within an organisation for a reason – but do they really understand that reason? Does everyone else see the role and the reason for it the same way? Why am I in this job? Why are our teams set up this way – can I see the sense in this? Structures can support or hinder working with purpose.

The Philosophy
People need to understand their organisation's purpose to value it, and their role within it.

...With Purpose...

n. reason for which something is done or exists; determination; practical advantage or use

If you're a fan of TED talks, you'll no doubt have seen Simon Sinek's seminal "Start With Why" (if not, search on YouTube[1]).

Again, it seems so simple – start your thinking and fixing with "why?".

But what happens if we ask people across our business what their purpose is, and what the purpose of the business is? Unless we've worked hard on this, I can almost guarantee you that you'll get a mish-mash of woolly answers that are part corporate mission statement, part job description, part personal driver and quite possibly partly ironic.

The trick with purpose is to make it as simple as possible if you want it the be clear and effective. Use short words. Tap into emotions.

And it's not all about profit. It's more about what matters to us as people. Our purpose is more about the values, drivers and objectives we have in serving our customers. Get that right and the profit will follow.

But purpose is not something we can decree from on high and expect everyone to slavishly follow. Purpose is about belief – shared values, shared drivers and shared objectives. Committed leadership, perhaps.

Purpose is also a key part of changes and outcomes. Why are we doing this? Why can we not go on as we are? Why is that? Do we believe that the effort to make the change will give us the outcome we want – and will anyone care?

The Philosophy

Purpose is a team game. Purpose creates your team's legacy. Purpose is the value that creates profit.

---

[1] https://www.youtube.com/watch?v=u4ZoJKF_VuA [pen & flipchart = multi-media!]

Part One – The Philosophies

...That Sells...

Selling is taking likely buyers through a building of desire and trust.

In a business, that enables us to make money by getting the commitment to buy.

In a public sector or charity, "selling" is about getting people to commit to take the action that matters to us – it's about convincing people to cross a threshold to take action: donating, writing a letter or similar.

That means knowing our buyers. Our audience. Our segment. Our tribe.

How are they defined? How do they see themselves? Why do they have that view? How does our team see the buyers? Are these views congruent? Are our people seeing the buyers the way they see themselves?

Are we making assumptions? (You know what they say about assumptions...)

I also use "desire" rather than "need", as let's face it, most buying decisions involve the heart as well as the head (or instead of).

Buyers pay us money, or make a commitment, when they have a compulsion. When a threshold has been crossed, or an event has taken place. When pressure gets too much to resist.

I talk about desire as a compulsion, but it also has a negative equivalent, in fear or revulsion. If these are at play, can we assure people that we can remove the fear or negative pressure?

Are we clear on those thresholds, events or pressures?

Do we know how they propagate through our processes, our business, our people, so that we understand what buyers need and how they feel about it?

When someone has a burning desire, they then need someone they really trust to meet that desire. If a need is commoditised or transactional, the trust needed is low, and loyalty doesn't matter.

If a buyer has a need they really feel passionate about (their own purpose), then often they seek someone who shares that passion (and purpose) to provide them with a solution.

What do you do to make every business interaction with your buyers about building either desire or trust, or both?

Selling is about making a promise. We make a promise that we can be trusted to provide something that satiates the buyer's desire.

How can your buyers trust you? What makes them loyal and confident?

Delivery, quality, evidence, track record? Rapport, empathy, congruency? Making realistic promises that you deliver upon? Sharing genuine interest?

The Philosophy
Selling successfully means everyone in the business helps build desire and trust in buyers.

...Products Or Services...

A product or service is not just a collection of things, or a series of activities. Our product or service makes a proposition: an offer to make a transformation to our buyer. We'll change their life physically or emotionally.

Is that how we see ourselves? Transformational? Do our people believe that? Do we talk in these terms with customers, whatever role we're in? Why would people use us to help them transform?

From a customer's point of view, what we offer is only the product or service they bought if it delivers upon its promise. Has it matched their quality expectations? Has it delivered what they needed? Has it sated the desire that they trusted us to meet?

How can we describe our product or service in these terms; of quality, fit to needs, meeting desires? Does everyone in the sales and delivery chain, and in the admin of our business, understand and believe in how their role creates the transformations we promise?

Nor can we exist in isolation – most organisations face competition. Even "do nothing" is a form of competition.

As we propose transformations that we can take our potential buyers through, so do our competitors, known and unknown. The market changes around us. Our competition make changes and advances we don't know about. They develop or reveal weaknesses we don't know about.

We must innovate to survive and thrive.

We need to give our customers "new reasons why" to engage with our offerings.

Innovation is the introduction of new ideas and methods – turning intangible thoughts into measurable action and material things.

How do we innovate in our business? Is it conscious, planned? Is it a result of eureka moments and happenstance? Or a mixture of both? Is it reactive, in a constant battle *against* change?

Innovation is driven by learning and experimenting.

Listening to feedback, engaging with excitement and frustration, mixing emotion with metrics. Letting the little things fail fast, to get to the big successes faster.

It's about accepting that failure is a necessary part of re-invention. It's about having a mindset and systems in place to help us continuously challenge our products and services to be better. We can make them better by understanding the "because" of their success or failure.

And that starts with knowing what better needs to look like. How will we move the game on by making bigger, better, or unexpected transformations for our customers?

When we know our customers – their purpose and ours – then we can help them solve problems they didn't even realise they had. We can build desire for things that don't yet exist, so we're the only business that can be trusted to deliver on that desire.

The Philosophy
Everyone in the business needs to feel responsible for transforming a clear part of the buyer's life.

...To Make A Profit

Hold on! I've already said that I believe the primary purpose of a business **shouldn't** be to make a profit – the profit should be the *result* of the purpose.

However, I could perhaps call profit a "prerequisite" for a business. No profit equals no business. Eventually, anyway. Profit is vital.

Profit is not a dirty word. How we make profit and what we do with it deals with the moral and ethical side of things. That's up to us and our people – and our buyers' and market's responses.

Even if we are a not-for-profit organisation, or charity, we can't operate at a deficit to our income and stay sustainable. So the same mentality applies – we need to create more value than the costs we incur.

And in its most basic form, of course, that's what profit is – the difference between our income and our costs.

As anyone who has been in business knows however, the reality of staying profitable can be much more nuanced (on a good day) or can feel almost impossible (on a bad day).

Breaking value/income and costs/expenditure down reveals a multitude of variables; not just the tangibles like materials, services and expenses but the more ethereal costs of time, delays, wastage, errors and rework.

These are some of the things I've learned and considered over the years. I continue to learn!

For many businesses I've worked with, time is the biggest cost. Paying salaries or holding stock for periods of time all cost.

These are easily measurable.

Well, usually fairly easily measurable.

Sometimes.

We think...

It's surprising how many times the assumed or perceived reality is different to the actual numbers.

Even people familiar with a process will often estimate (or guess) times and costs that are out in some key areas. Little wonder then, that managers and staff end up at loggerheads over resources assigned to key process steps. This lack of clarity also feeds into distrust and feeling misunderstood (we question one another's purpose in discussions about efficiency, for example).

Costs in materials and expenses can be crippling for capital intensive businesses (manufacturing, retail, etc.). Even services-based businesses can build up a surprising spend on expenses in particular – and to what end? Are the expenses helping the desire, trust and transformations for customers? Are they helping staff feel like they are working to a core purpose, or are they evidence of family meals missed, weekends lost to fatigue, and tours of airport lounges?

If costs are the expenditure we can't really avoid, then wastage, delays, duplication and rework are the unforgivable spending. They really punish our business, people and ultimately customers, as they hit the bottom line, hard.

Perhaps the most frustrating thing is that they are often only spotted after the fact – they are "lag" metrics; measurable things that have already happened. Money already spent, budget already burned. People pat themselves on the back for rescuing a situation with effort and emergency spending, saying never again. Until the next time. Until the last straw is spotted on the latest P&L report or management accounts.

Time wasted on delays, mistakes and duplication is also not available to other tasks – usually the ones that are more rewarding, like working with customers or colleagues, or innovating new offerings. As well as the hit on costs, there's the impact on capability, resiliency and morale.

Let's get more positive – the income side of profit.

We need to get our value across really clearly to buyers. If we are completely trusted to fully meet their desires, then they will pay more – what they believe is fair for the value, for the transformation.

We also need to look at supply and demand; and scaling our offering versus preserving its scarcity.

We need to look at what it is buyers value about our proposition. Is it the quality of the materials we use? Is it the way we make them feel with the service we provide and the expense we go to, to make them feel valued? Is it about how reliable we are – right first time, every time? Is it about our turnaround time? Is it about the fact that we take time to listen to them and build rapport? Is it about the fact that we don't keep asking them to repeat themselves every time they speak to someone new in the business? Why do they value us, or not?

These are all bits of our value proposition that can be mapped right back to our cost components. That helps us make sure we have a healthy gap between value created and costs accrued. Keeping the customer's desire at the heart of things also helps with keeping a clear sense of purpose.

Why does this matter?

Priority.

Don't fix first what people don't value. Conversely, don't leave to chance the things that matter to our buyers. Don't analyse and fix the "obvious" things, fix the things that matter. Fix what builds desire, trust and transformation.

We can't leave profitability without touching on cashflow. Bad cashflow can kill good businesses. Growth can stretch cashflow. So growth can kill good businesses. (Yes, I know, some days it feels like lots of things can kill good businesses!)

I think that timing plays a big role here. Not just "how long does it take to get paid", but frequency: how often do we model, track and review the financials? There's also the absolute timing of events. When is the right time to get investment for growth? When should we launch a new product? When should we take staff on? Lose staff? Get customers? Sack customers?

Profit. For such a short word, there's a lot to consider, track, control and improve.

The Philosophy
People need to feel accountable for the costs and value they create for the business and buyers

4 People And Purpose

I hope that one of the things that comes across so far is that I believe people are at the centre of running and improving businesses. No real surprise there, I guess.

But collecting and summarising my experience in The Flow of Purpose underlined to me why purpose must flow through your organisation; for it to succeed, adapt and prosper.

Not only that, but purpose must connect you and your people with your customers (or service users or citizens – whoever uses what you do).

Let's recap some definitions and then the five basic philosophies of The Flow of Purpose.

What Is Purpose?

- Purpose n. reason for which something is done or exists; determination; practical advantage or use

What Is A Business?

- My definition: An organisation with purpose that sells products or services to make a profit.

The Five Philosophies of The Flow Purpose

- People need to understand their organisation's purpose to value it, and their role within it.
- Purpose is a team game. Purpose creates your team's legacy. Purpose is the value that creates profit.
- Selling successfully means everyone in the business helps build desire and trust in buyers.
- Everyone in the business needs to feel responsible for transforming a clear part of the buyer's life.
- People need to feel accountable for the costs and value they create for the business and buyers.

Leading Our People

If we want to analyse and improve our businesses, do a better job for buyers and grow and prosper, we need to find ways to connect people with things like:

- Purpose
- Value
- Role
- Relationships
- Buyers
- Desire and trust
- Responsibility
- Transformation

- Accountability
- Costs.

As you'd expect, at the head of the list is purpose. It gives meaning to all the other areas. Purpose, the "why", must flow through the what, how, when, where and who of your organisation.

People need to believe in why they come to work in the morning. Why they persevere through challenges, why innovation & improvement is so important. Why it's important to delight customers and feel the pain of a customer that feels let down. Why we all need to work together, however hard it feels at times. Why sometimes, people need to change.

The Flow of Purpose means we all matter to one another and to the customer; and they to us. What's the alternative? Irrelevance.

OK, But What About Practicalities?

That's good, but we need practical action to turn the warm and fuzzy positivity of purpose into new ways of working. I've boiled years of learning, guidance, experience, experimentation, failure and re-design into four simple stages that I use to bring people together to improve businesses and create a purpose-driven plan to follow.

They are inclusive, interactive and effective. They build upon four simple diagrams as the anchor for wider discussion and debate. They encourage people to examine how and why we work together. They encourage collaboration.

Sounds great, right?

They also help expose differences, arguments, dissatisfaction and frustrations that you may not have seen before.

Good. If we know the negatives, if people trust us enough to share the problems, then we can address them with new thinking, shared ideas, and a team that cares. We help The Flow of Purpose to do its work. When you debate purpose with people, be prepared for things to get heated at times. We're challenging what people care about. Some sacred cows could end up becoming endangered species...

Part One – The Philosophies

Before we look at the practicalities of using the four diagrams, let's spend a little longer digging into the aspects of our business we covered above.

Let's prepare ourselves to improve our businesses with purpose, by exploring questions we might ask.

Part Two – The Preparation

- Introduction
- The Philosophies
- **The Preparation**
- The Practicalities
- Share Priorities
- Find Stakeholders
- Explore Processes
- Purposeful Planning

Part Two – The Preparation

5 Why Take Time To Prepare?

If you're pushed for time, you can skip right ahead to Part Three – The Practicalities; but I hope you'll take some time to go through this section, whether now or after you've read part Three.

Part Two is about mind-set. I'm going to expand on the points and philosophies from Part One. In this part of The Flow of Purpose, I'm coming more from the standpoint of structured curiosity than philosophy. I want to share with you some of the experiences I've had in the different areas that contribute to the five philosophies I identified.

I don't expect my experiences and ideas will completely mirror yours. There will be as much to question or disagree with as there is to nod along to as you read. Once again, this is not a bad thing. What I want to do is to provide a loose framework of topics, and some seed-thinking from my own experience to help you identify the questions you feel you want to ask in, around and about your organisation.

This section is basically a checklist of questions for you to consider and contemplate before launching into analysis – especially if you are pulling your team around you to do so. It helps you build some context before turning on the taps of team input and grabbing the monkey wrench of the practical tools...

After each section in Part Two, I finish with the same six questions. After the thinking and brainstorming of each set of experiences and questions, answering these questions can help you identify key areas and priorities to analyse with the tools in Part Three.

Let's get to it.

Quality Time Is Rarely Wasted

There's a common theme that comes up time and again when I do consulting and analysis projects.

After interviews or workshops, people will often tell me "that was really useful, we just don't get the time to discuss what we do and how we improve it" or something similar.

It feels like "thinking of our situation" is not seen as valuable compared to being "on the tools" or in meetings or talking to customers or suppliers.

So how exactly do we expect improvements to happen? Magic?

One of the first things any business coach will challenge a business owner with is "are you spending time working *in* your business, or working *on* your business?"

Improvements come from working on our business, not in it. By looking at it with an outsider's eyes and fixing problems we see.

Taking time to explore and think about our situation, possible root causes and options is the start point of analysing, creating ideas (ideation), and implementing solutions. OK, so the whole point of a business analysis and improvement project is to do that (find problems and implement solutions). But here, what I'm talking about is a bit of ground work before you start the main project.

Part Two – The Preparation

Analyst Heal Thyself. A Bit.

Research supports the old saying that a problem shared is a problem halved[2]. Just sharing a situation and finding the words to describe it to someone can help with identifying and fixing the underlying problem.

In much the same way, just running through this part of the book and jotting down notes on where you think you are is a valuable start.

You'll have some clarity for yourself on where things stand across your role, team and business. A bit of a steer on priority, driven by gut feel if nothing else.

If you make notes as you read, you'll have a list of assumptions to be evidenced and opinions to be challenged. So, rather than starting your team sessions with a blank sheet of paper (always a slow start), you'll have some points for people to argue for and against. Points to jump off from into other areas.

You may not agree with all the items I've included in this section. You'll probably add a few that I've missed but which are vital for your organisation.

Great. Own this list, make it yours.

Even better, in future make it your team's list. Or your business's. What about looking at the list through the customers' eyes, or suppliers'? Dare you invite customers to comment on each area?

Don't worry if you don't have an answer to everything (or have more answers than questions). These are just points to get you thinking – preparatory brainstorming, if you like.

As you think about each section, if you try to describe your current situation and aspirations, what does that tell you about your business? How does that make you feel? How might others be feeling about that area?

Is there clear purpose or meaning within each area, or behind each situation?

---

[2] Sarah Townsend, Heejung Kim, Batja Mesquita (2014) "Are you Feeling what I'm Feeling? Emotional Similarity Buffers Stress" Social Psychological and Personality Science 5, 526-533.

6 Exploring The Organisation

Our core philosophy here is:

People need to understand their organisation's purpose to value it, and their role within it.

The Organisation – People, Skills & Structure

Introduction

On the surface, people, skills and structure is simply about having people in the right jobs, organised for efficiency and effectiveness, to manage authority, responsibility and accountability, and get work done.

If only life were that simple. People and organisation are also about politics, fiefdoms, matrix-responsibilities, assumed responsibilities, sloping-shoulders, duplicated roles, noses put out of joint, differing standards of leadership, nicer desks than ours, offices too cold/too hot, different approaches to signing off expenses, slimy sales people versus pedantic technicians, off days, sick days, holiday arguments, hangovers, heroic all-nighters, office bust-ups and pulling together. Complicated, in other words.

Being clearer on a common purpose across all parts of our business is never going to stop these from happening, let's be clear. But what it can do is help with defusing and fixing some of these situations. A flow of purpose makes it clear that we're all on the same side, for the same reason. So the argument is worth solving.

Here are some other things to consider...

Questions To Ponder

Do we have an organisation chart? Is it up to date? Has anyone ever used it? Does it reflect reality?

Does our structure work for us or against us, when it comes to delivering transformation to customers? Why is that the case? Is the structure there for some other reason, like regulatory compliance?

Can staff identify and reach the people, skills and authority they need, when they need to? Can we?

How do people know when to escalate situations and delegate work? Does everyone share that view of the criteria?

Do customers and suppliers understand how we work when they call or meet us with a query or problem?

How much do titles and positions matter to the business and to people? What motivates people? What demotivates them? How do we know for sure? How do we affect motivation?

How do we go about making sure that the right skills are used for the right tasks at the right time?

How do we train people? How do we grow their experience? How do we "quality control" people's skills?

Do we have pockets of under-used skills or over-stretched experts? Are these short-term or long-term situations? Why have these situations happened? What can be done about them, potentially?

How can we get people with the right skills in the right roles in the right proportions? Can we change the nature of the skills need – change the job, outsource, stop providing a loss-making service, change the price to allow us to use contractors, etc?

How do we manage performance to encourage excellent or appropriate outcomes? How do we spot out of line situations – and can/do we nip them in the bud, catch them in time or have constant rescue missions after car-crash situations?

Your Notes And Contemplations

- What has come out of your musings on these areas?
- What questions have been raised in your mind about fit with the organisation's purpose?
- What facts can you note down (what's your evidence)?
- What assumptions can you validate with your team, peers or colleagues?
- What do you feel you need to understand (analyse) better?
- What do you feel compelled to fix or address? Why?

The Organisation – Processes

Introduction

A good (but often unexpected) place to start talking about internal processes is the customer.

Consider the situation from your own, personal point of view.

Let's say you buy a product or service from a business to solve a problem and are really happy with it. You rave about it, recommend it, and a close friend with the same issue rushes out to buy the same product or service, full of expectation...

(You can probably see where this is going...)

If your friend gets the same excellent result as you, then happy days. Same need, same result, same delight. Another recommendation too, probably.

If however the experience is awful – the buying process was handled differently – then you may end up with one less friend, one less card to buy at Christmas, and possibly a mangled widget violently deposited on your front lawn.

The serious point here is that customers feel really let down when they get variable service. Sometimes I think people feel more let down by variable service than consistently poor service. If your processes are not working well, especially customer-focused ones, then you will have unhappy customers or staff, or both. Measure satisfaction if you think that's not true. Broken processes also hurt staff morale, because they often involve extra effort, manual fixes, workarounds and doing things twice. They also bring the wearying pain of clearly letting people down.

On the flip side, I'm often surprised at how just assembling people to talk about process pains and possibilities finds simple fixes. A new field on a form, one person or role knowing they're responsible for a specific decision, colour-coded bags, morning meetings – these are all fixes that have come out of group sessions I've helped with. In some cases, they have doubled or tripled process productivity.

Questions to Ponder

Do we need or have a process manual, or some form of document that explains how we work? What's an appropriate scale/format for our business now? What about if we are growing?

If we have process documentation, does anyone care? Who, why? Can it be made more accessible, especially common or emergency procedures (think airline safety cards)?

How do people know what processes they're involved in? How do they place their role within a process?

How do/can/would we visualise our processes – can we visualise them, map them out, or show them as a task list? How often does the process fit, and how often are we dealing with "special cases"?

Do people feel empowered to suggest (or make) process improvements? How do they know that? When was the last time someone did so? Who supported them? What was the result? How did they benefit? What about the business? The customer?

How would we on-board a new employee so that they work in the right ways for our business? (A great test of our documentation quality).

How would we go about identifying a problem process – a blockage or delay, or the point where the product or service keeps going wrong? What prompts us to do this? How often do/should we do this?

If needed, can we relate processes to policies and to legislation, if needed, for compliance? How could we prove to an auditor that important things are done the right way?

Do we have enough process documentation? Do we have too much process documentation? The right number of documents, but the wrong level of detail? What about format? Would other roles agree with our assessment? If they feel unwieldy, are individual processes too big? Consider – a hospital A&E (ER) deals with more unknowns than most businesses, but is kept safe with sets of rigorous procedures.

Do people value repeatable results from processes? Is such repeatability a valid concept in our organisation? Is consistency valued?

Do our processes start and end with customers? If not, can people clearly see how a process relates to the customer – something they need or are involved in?

Your Notes And Contemplations

- What has come out of your musings on these areas?
- What questions have been raised in your mind about fit with the organisation's purpose?
- What facts can you note down (what's your evidence)?
- What assumptions can you validate with your team, peers or colleagues?
- What do you feel you need to understand (analyse) better?
- What do you feel compelled to fix or address? Why?

Part Two – The Preparation

The Organisation – Systems

Introduction

If processes are the methods of doing things, then systems are the moving parts that embody the methods. Process and Systems = Instructions and Tools.

And we all know what happens if we use tools without reading the instructions. You can get away with it with a hammer, but probably not with a life support machine.

Before we build and use tools, we really need to know what they're going to do for us. Inputs, steps and outputs. Organise before we systemise. Start with the purpose of the system and the process.

Another one of those things that sounds simple, but often proves difficult. I believe there are several reasons for this.

We can design a perfect process and system for today, but tomorrow will bring new challenges. The system either fails to meet them, or clever people think up novel workarounds (re-using data fields for other purposes is a classic). Scope has changed without anyone really knowing.

It could be that we try to get too much into one system. We have to then use it well enough, for long enough, to get the return on our investment. Unless we're lucky or careful when we spec the system, we're trapped with one monolithic way of working.

We might systemise when we should keep it manual, or struggle on with manual tasks buried somewhere in a remote office that really should be systemised. Systemise the routine, humanise the exceptions.

With IT and computer systems, we then get into the whole thing about on-premise or cloud. More on that below...

From the point of view of The Flow of Purpose, systems are the tools that make it quicker, easier and more repeatable for us to carry out our work with purpose.

Questions to Ponder

Do we know what systems our business uses – do we have a list? Does that list include the central spreadsheet Phil in accounts created to form the basis of production line job numbers? The web app that Abbie pulled together to query engineer availability for the customer portal? The paper form that Goods Out use to know what to send as a priority?

Is it clear for each system how they fit in to the purpose of each role? Do people understand why it's important that they use each system properly? Is it actually important?

What would happen if we lost a system? Who would care? What would suffer, who would be affected? How long would it take to remedy the issue? Could we fix it (are there obsolete parts or components needed)?

If we need to change things, can we break systems down into components?

Can (should?) we combine similar systems together if they share a similar purpose (common in companies that have been through mergers – big systems like CRM tend to get done during the merger, but smaller systems often survive for years)?

What limitations do we feel or know our systems create for us? Why? How does that make it difficult for roles to play their part in meaningful work?

How easy is it for people to trace through and understand the impact of changes they may want to systems? Do we have processes in place to manage the debate between competing stakeholder needs? Constructively?

Is your IT on-site, in the cloud or a hybrid of the two? What do we think are the operational, risk, compliance and cost aspects of this situation? What about availability, resiliency, scalability, accessibility? Data ownership and security? Does our workforce demographic affect our decisions on technologies?

If someone else provides systems to us, do we or they measure the effectiveness? Have we kept hold of management and control, or outsourced it too? Does that matter, for any given system?

Part Two – The Preparation

Your Notes And Contemplations

- What has come out of your musings on these areas?
- What questions have been raised in your mind about fit with the organisation's purpose?
- What facts can you note down (what's your evidence)?
- What assumptions can you validate with your team, peers or colleagues?
- What do you feel you need to understand (analyse) better?
- What do you feel compelled to fix or address? Why?

Part Two – The Preparation

7 Exploring Purpose

Our core philosophy here is:

Purpose is a team game. Purpose creates your team's legacy. Purpose is the value that creates profit.

Purpose – The Big Why

Introduction

I believe that the idea of a "flow of purpose" is compelling and powerful. It ties different stakeholders across an organisation together through making each job and task meaningful.

It's a simple idea. That doesn't mean it's easy.

I sometimes use the analogy of climbing a mountain like Kilimanjaro.

It's simple to climb a mountain. You put one foot in front of the other until you reach the top.

That doesn't make it easy.

Some steps are harder than others. Sometimes we're on our knees scrabbling through the scree. Sometimes we need a rope or crampons. And don't forget that some amazing people climb mountains blind, in wheelchairs or with prosthetics. It's the same with purpose – we can't assume the flow is as smooth for others as we might see it.

The first challenge we have is to define our purpose. One that everyone can buy into. This is normally harder than it sounds. However, it is the foundation of sustainable business improvement and growth. It's worth investing time in. We'll look at how to do this more in Part Three.

When we have our clear purpose, we need to work out how we get people to believe in it, and to believe in it applying to their role, every day. It needs to mean something to them, and the people they interact with. It's also about respecting each other's contributions to our purpose.

And we finish off by making the purpose a habit, part of our day-to-day, part of our culture.

Questions to Ponder

Do we already have a clear purpose for the organisation? Shorter than a mission statement; maybe a well-written vision statement? Does anyone know it? Do they live by it?

Do people feel part of something? Do they believe their role, no matter how small, matters in getting the overall job done? How do they gauge that? How do we know that people feel part of something? Are we assuming a level of understanding or clarity that isn't there?

Is there a consistent purpose across the organisation (or parts of it) that is perhaps unwritten, but strong? Do you already have purpose flowing in parts of your organisation? If so, why is that (strong leader, clear processes, tight-knit team, etc.)?

Is our organisation comfortable with debating the conceptual, or do we need to cross some sort of "fluffy woo-woo Rubicon" before we talk about the purpose and meaning of one's role and the flow of some nebulous purpose stuff? (Let's be realistic about how we pitch this to people). Do we need to talk about "only doing things that matter" rather than "The Flow of Purpose"? What version of "the big why" will get us the best reaction and buy-in?

If we had an employee in front of us, could they describe a link between their key tasks and the customer having a rewarding experience – a desire/trust transformation?

Do we know what our own people (our staff, colleagues) want? What are their desires and trust needs for their own roles, teams and departments? Internal customers are customers nonetheless. Can we define a purpose that connects what we want each day with what our customers want?

What forum or platform do we have to discuss purpose? Can we piggyback on existing meetings and communications mechanisms? Or, will we be better to set up some new meetings, workshops, working groups or collaboration tools?

Your Notes And Contemplations

- What has come out of your musings on these areas?
- What questions have been raised in your mind about fit with the organisation's purpose?
- What facts can you note down (what's your evidence)?
- What assumptions can you validate with your team, peers or colleagues?
- What do you feel you need to understand (analyse) better?
- What do you feel compelled to fix or address? Why?

Purpose – Changes and Outcomes

Introduction

Why does change happen? Does it need to happen?

Wait long enough, and ageing happens. Very little stays static in the long-term. So even if we think things aren't changing, they are. Ageing is change due to the passage of time, which is kind of tricky to control. But we need to deal with its effects. That's why reading glasses exist.

If we're talking change in the context of The Flow of Purpose, it's change for a reason. Reaction to a stimulus. Whether that stimulus is time, events or strategy, we're dealing with change, and we need to think about outcomes.

Part Two – The Preparation

It's a commonly held belief that people in general don't like change. But is that the whole story? If we're creating better outcomes **together**, does that change the way that people see change? If people feel like they're making changes rather than suffering from change, does that change the sense of purpose? Does it turn grumbles into acceptance rather than blocking?[3]

One of the main reasons we analyse businesses, strategies or processes is to change them.

I've done a lot of such analysis work over the years. People coming into analysis meetings and interviews vary in attitude from excited through to hostile. I've also seen pretty much every emotion in between as well, from fear and concern to apathy and cynicism.

In most cases, you can bring people round to contributing positively, but it can take time.

It normally also needs evidence that the outcomes we allude to can be or are being delivered.

But, I find one of the most effective things you can do is make people actively want to participate in change. Sharing a clear, powerful purpose helps immensely here.

Outcomes are the other side of change.

The case for change is often described in terms of new outcomes after reacting to the stimulus and making the change.

Change, outcomes and purpose are interesting things to consider together. Something can happen (a change) that leads to an outcome that affects our purpose – our reasons for doing things. Or, we can choose a new purpose to justify changes and a new outcome.

For example, in the first case, we might provide compliance-related services to help clients stay legal. Then the law changes to give our clients direct web access to government-held information, as part of the state's digital transformation agenda. That law change has removed a huge amount of the value-add outcome that we previously provided. Customers will no longer

---

[3] This (old) Harvard Business Review article has some interesting points on change: https://hbr.org/1969/01/how-to-deal-with-resistance-to-change - 1969! plus ça change, plus c'est la même chose, eh?!

see our value, meaning or purpose in that area. External factors have reduced or removed our purpose. To survive and prosper, we need to find new ways to be meaningful and get all of our people working in new ways.

A second example of change and outcome is choosing a new purpose. Suppose we run an IT team in a reasonable sized business, which has an overall purpose of giving customers up-to-the-minute financial information, so they can get market-beating returns. The strategic decision has been made to adopt Office 365 or Google Docs, and move application workloads to AWS. To avoid losing the wealth of skill and experience in the IT team, we might choose to "repurpose" from providing reliable infrastructure to providing a deeper level of support for business intelligence, and faster, more personal support to individuals. This is the classic IT idea of switching from 70% fix vs 30% value-add to 30% fixing and 70% creating value. The purpose of the IT team changes from fixing things that delay up-to-the-minute information to building new ways to find and deliver insight as part of the greater purpose.

Questions to Ponder

Is our purpose driving the outcomes and changes, or have events meant our purpose has been affected? Do people across the organisation understand the relationship between changes, outcomes and purpose?

How do we manage change in our organisation? Who is responsible for change? How formal does change management need to be?

How successful are we as an organisation at making changes? Are there parts of the organisation that are better (or worse) than others at handling change? What makes them different?

How do we go about understanding the outcomes of change? Do we have business cases? What compulsions or thresholds do we have? Do we consider risks? Do we track risks? How regularly? No, really, how regularly?

What is an appropriate level of involvement (for our organisation) of general staff in change exploration and management?

How do we assess the potential impact of change? Do we model it? Draw it out? Discuss it? Try it in a test environment? JFDI (just do it)?

How do we find, engage and inform stakeholders who might be impacted by a change? How confident are we that we haven't missed anyone?

How much warning do we give people of change? Staff? Customers?

Do we have a rollback plan in place? A fall-back or workaround if it all goes castors-up? Who calls the shots on these at what points in the change process? Why – how are these sorts of decisions related to our purpose?

Do people understand the purpose of changes – how do we get that across to them? How do we check that they'll support rather than block?

Do we understand the "softer impacts" of change on how people go about their days? Might people feel neglected or taken for granted through change, even if they "get" the logic of the situation? Are people likely to be enthusiastic or suspicious of changes?

Do people get a chance to influence the change or outcomes? Will they feel that their purpose and role is being considered through the change? Is that something we can do, or do we need to be honest with people and say we're pushing forward with a change without their input? If so, have we explained why?

How do we tend to support people through and after change? How long do we give people to realise we were serious when we said the change would happen, and they need to learn things, get to grips with new things and adopt them as habits?

Do we measure the actual results of changes and look back at what we thought would happen?

If we have been bitten by the law of unintended consequences, what caused this? Can we do something to stop similar things happening again? What were the root causes? Could someone else reasonably been expected to spot the issue if they'd been involved (different viewpoint)?

How do we capture the things we've learned? How formally do we record these? Does the approach work well enough?

Your Notes And Contemplations

- What has come out of your musings on these areas?
- What questions have been raised in your mind about fit with the organisation's purpose?
- What facts can you note down (what's your evidence)?
- What assumptions can you validate with your team, peers or colleagues?
- What do you feel you need to understand (analyse) better?
- What do you feel compelled to fix or address? Why?

Purpose – Attitude and Culture

Introduction
Attitude

My personal philosophy is to recruit for attitude above skill. Skills can be taught, but attitude is much harder to change, in my experience.

So what is attitude, in terms of The Flow of Purpose? This is something you need to define for yourselves as an organisation, but let me share some ideas. To help purpose flow and prosper, with "attitude," I look for things like:

- Being positively curious, not just accepting the status quo – *why* do things happen or get said?
- Caring about outcomes for others as well as oneself – do impacts match needs & expectations?
- Willingness to discuss things openly, whether comfortable or not – have we shared the "true why?"
- An ability to listen – and truly take in *intent* as well as what is actually said.
- Knowing when to empathise and build rapport; and knowing when to stand back.

I've evolved my criteria for bringing new people into my teams to three principles:

- Be a miniature force of nature.
- Have the confidence to engage in constructive debate.
- Have the humility to listen and learn every day.

Why do I use these three rules?

A miniature force of nature could mean someone is like a hurricane, bringing massive, whirling energy to shake things up and look in and under everything. It could mean they are like tectonic plates, using irresistible, inexorable effort to move mountains and change the landscape. They could be a lightning storm, with crackling energy that illuminates things whilst delivering the energy to make change. Or, they could be like a river, ceaselessly working through obstacles, finding ways over and through things, able to change whole landscapes in time.

What force of nature might you be? Can you look around your team and give them each a force? How can you harness that?

I prefer a confidence that stops well short of arrogance, but I do look for people who are willing to argue for what they feel is right. Now, that doesn't mean I always want people to be right (see rule 3!). However, working constructively through healthy debate, creative tension, or opposing viewpoints is often a great way to get to the true "why" of a situation. Often, the options for mutual gain and new and creative solutions are seeded in such debates. When done positively, this is so powerful. It can also be difficult to keep debates professional if there is a lot at stake; so this rule is not as easy to fulfil as we might initially think. I look for people who respect others' purposes.

"Listen and learn" is another rule that sounds obvious. That said, I find there is a tension when I am brought in to a situation to advise and be a consultant. I need to prove and deliver my value, which may be bringing deep experience and insight to bear; I can't just ask a load of questions. But if I ask the *right* questions, born of experience, I can both bring insight to clients, and learn things myself. So I must bring both questions and answers. The tricky bit is bringing the right questions and answers in the perception of the client... Mostly, this rule is about finding people who care. They put themselves in the other person's shoes and asks "what do I need to learn, what could I do, what would I do in their shoes?"

Culture

I read a great line once (I wish I could remember where), which went something like "your culture is set when you take on your first employee". Another concept that made me really think is that "your culture is how people behave when the boss isn't around". That's perhaps quite a cynical or sardonic way of looking at it, but I find it strangely compelling – what does that say about me!?

Culture exists in organisations, whether we define and express it formally or not. From the two examples above, you can probably see that I think there's merit in consciously planning and communicating culture, well in advance of growth if you can.

I think that culture links very strongly with The Flow of Purpose; one might even say that The Flow of Purpose philosophies (or better, your flavours of them) could be part of a cultural blueprint.

Your culture is the lens through which your policies, processes and practices are viewed, operated and scrutinised. Culture is "organisational attitude".

Like so many things, culture takes a long time to get right, and just one bad hire to poison. Knowing this means you can recruit, review and implement with a positive, purposeful culture in mind.

Questions to Ponder

Have we identified and written down what attitude is needed, where, in your organisation? Why did we decide on these components of attitude? How do they fit our purpose?

If we had to go round all of our departments, teams and people, and pick three words to describe their attitude, what would the words be? What does that tell us about them? Are there patterns and/or inconsistencies?

Do the different attitudes we identify create friction between teams, or factions across the business?

Do we have attitude questions in our recruitment and promotion reviews? How can people evidence their attitude, and how it fits with our organisation? We need to be fair (and legal) to candidates and staff if we're using attitude to make hiring/advancement decisions.

How do people know what attitude the organisation values? The attitudes that don't go down well? How can people learn and improve themselves?

Is our culture documented anywhere? Do people live and breathe it?

How would we describe our organisation's culture? Would others say the same? Are there different cultures in different areas? Does that create conflict or opportunities? How do we know?

If we've been through mergers or acquisitions, have the cultures been aligned, or is there respect between them?

How would our clients describe our culture, from what they've seen? How would our staff describe it? Are they the same? Are we willing to ask this question of clients and staff for real? If not, what worries us?

What do we want our culture to be? How do we think we'll communicate, inspire and enforce it?

Do we have any people or teams that are not living the culture? Why not? What can we do to inspire, educate and align them?

Who are the leaders in our organisation? Formal and informal? How effective are they? Why do people follow them? A sense of shared meaning/purpose or morbid curiosity...?

What's our approach to management of people; day-to-day (operational), personal growth, etc.?

Your Notes And Contemplations

- What has come out of your musings on these areas?
- What questions have been raised in your mind about fit with the organisation's purpose?
- What facts can you note down (what's your evidence)?
- What assumptions can you validate with your team, peers or colleagues?
- What do you feel you need to understand (analyse) better?
- What do you feel compelled to fix or address? Why?

8 Exploring Selling

Our core philosophy here is:

Selling successfully means everyone in the business helps build desire and trust in buyers.

Selling – Desire & Trust

Introduction

At its most basic level, buying and selling only happens when someone has sufficient desire for an outcome, and enough trust that it will be delivered.

Or put another way, when buying, I want promise to be delivered upon. Whether that's an ice-cream or an ERP system. (Usually ice-cream for me).

In simple terms, desire usually comes from stopping a pain, or experiencing delight or distraction. However, I think there is also a threshold angle to consider. There needs to be a level of compulsion for someone to buy. That could be overwhelming immediate need, a gradual increase in need to beyond a trigger point, or some event that changes a state.

Even when adorned with the decorations of the corporate environment, these basic components of desire and trust are still there.

For desire in business, it could be that we need to reduce pain: stop errors happening, shorten delays, make more effective decisions, fight back against competitors taking market share, etc.

Or it could be delight – redesigning our offices to improve the working environment, getting a new website designed to showcase our new brand, markedly improving staff morale or customer satisfaction.

In business, trust most often comes from products, services or projects being delivered as we were told they would be.

Questions to Ponder

Do we know who our buyers are? Do we have avatars or personae for them – their profiles and back-stories? The history that drives their desires?

How do we understand the needs and desires of our typical buyers?

How do we understand their fears and pains?

What laws or compliance needs create a need in our market or area? How do we track these to prepare for changes in needs?

How much do different roles in our organisation feel connected with the end customer? Do people relate good or bad performance in their role with happy or disappointed customers?

How do we manage accountability for both selling and delivering?

Are people across the organisation proud of what we do for our customers? Why? If not, why not?

What ways do we have of measuring how much our customers trust us? Do we collect metrics, or just hope for low "churn"?

Your Notes And Contemplations
- What has come out of your musings on these areas?
- What questions have been raised in your mind about fit with the organisation's purpose?
- What facts can you note down (what's your evidence)?
- What assumptions can you validate with your team, peers or colleagues?

- What do you feel you need to understand (analyse) better?
- What do you feel compelled to fix or address? Why?

Selling – Your Buyers

Introduction

We can map desire and trust back to The Flow of Purpose. The link here is that wherever people are in your organisation, they need to feel that they are playing a part in desire and trust. Either they are helping make the right promises to buyers, delivering the promised outcomes, or both.

Our sales people make promises, our delivery and support people fulfil those promises.

So, to deliver against desire and promises, that means everyone in the delivery chain and supporting functions needs to have some insight into the customer's needs – their purpose.

And to sell things that we can be trusted to deliver, means the people selling need to understanding the realistic extent and impact of what we can do for the customer – how we meet their purpose.

Knowing our customers' underlying purpose and drivers in detail helps to align what our people do with customer needs. Things like account management plans can help in this regard. These are formal documents which are written for each major client.

For each account (customer), account management plans provide e.g.:

- A pen portrait of who they are.
- What they stand for (purpose).
- Why, how and what they do for their customers.
- How what we do supports them.
- The nature, status and plans for our relationship with them as a customer.
- Our strategy and next actions with the customer, to meet our & their purposes.

There are of course many, many ways of engaging with customers, and these plans are but one idea. We need to decide what works best in our environment to help people feel like they are an essential part of customer success.

If we are a larger or more complex businesses, it might not be practical for our staff to understand the individual purposes of each customer. What we can do though, is educate our people in customer archetypes. These are real or theoretical customers that we use to explain why what each of us does has a part to play in The Flow of Purpose, and making promises we deliver upon. The main reason to do this is to make people think and keep them thinking. "Why does what I'm doing now really matter?"

Questions to Ponder

Do our sales and delivery people both understand that our business needs to make compelling promises it can realistically fulfil?

Do we have a way for delivery people to support sales people in making appropriate promises to customers? Could sales people be making bigger or bolder promises (because we have better things to offer)? Or, do they need to be more realistic with what we promise (because we have limits on what we can deliver)?

Have delivery people given adequate and accurate support to sales people when promises are made? We need to avoid "if only I'd been in the sales conversation..." type arguments.

Do delivery teams value the sales process? Do sales people value the delivery process? How do both sides of "the promise equation" fit to your overall business purpose?

Are sales staff "keeping anything back" in terms of what they know of the client's needs, attitudes, expectations, etc?

Are delivery staff honest and open early enough of problems in meeting promises?

Do we have any way of measuring the "hit rate" we have of successfully delivering against promises? What criteria or indicators do we use?

Do we have any problems with making and keeping promises? Are they systemic (i.e. they happen often or are widespread), or tied to individuals, companies, markets or products/services?

Your Notes And Contemplations

- What has come out of your musings on these areas?
- What questions have been raised in your mind about fit with the organisation's purpose?
- What facts can you note down (what's your evidence)?
- What assumptions can you validate with your team, peers or colleagues?
- What do you feel you need to understand (analyse) better?
- What do you feel compelled to fix or address? Why?

9 Exploring Propositions

Our core philosophy here is:

Everyone in the business needs to feel responsible for transforming a clear part of the buyer's life.

Products & Services – Propositions

Introduction

Your proposition is what convinces people to actually buy. A mediocre service or product with a compelling proposition will often outsell a great service or product with an unclear proposition.

A great proposition really speaks to the ideal buyer – inspiring them to see a transformation they will experience. A proposition is an offer that really means something. (Makes people want to say "I do!", I suppose...)

The proposition for your service or product is much more than just some sales collateral or a marketing campaign. Your proposition is the alignment of all the people and resources in your business behind delivering those amazing transformations.

Part Two – The Preparation

And yes, it can be difficult to get staff far away from one-to-one customer contact to feel they are part of a transformation. But, unless their job is actually unnecessary, they *are* part of the transformation. (And if their job truly is unnecessary, we have a different problem to worry about!)

This is partly why The Flow of Purpose digs into processes (in Part Three). We want to show our people how breaking or stopping just one seemingly small step can damage an entire customer transformation. Conversely, fixing one thing can have a big positive effect.

When it comes to communicating your proposition concisely, there are many formats for building sentences and short pitches. You can use structures like "verb-application-differentiator" or "verb-object-context", or the proposition structure from a book like Crossing the Chasm.[4]

However you approach your proposition, the main things are to make sure you have an audience that understands why they should engage with you, what they'll get, and how they take the next step with you.

Here are some quick examples from the web:

- Facebook helps you *connect and share* (verbs) with the *people* (object) *in your life* (context).
- Stripe is the best *software platform* (application) for *running* an internet business (verb). We handle *billions of dollars every year* for forward-thinking businesses around the world (differentiator).

Creating these short pitches is always an interesting exercise to try with a group of your own staff. See where there are similarities and differences, between groups/people, and between the propositions created and your corporate materials...

For The Flow of Purpose, there should be a sense of our work linking to the transformation for customers.

In the examples above, there is a sense that bringing people that matter to one another together makes a positive difference (Facebook example). For Stripe, the transformation feels like we are helping businesses be more

---

[4] "Crossing the Chasm: Marketing and Selling Disruptive Products to Mainstream Customers", Geoffrey A Moore, Collins Business Essentials

forward-thinking and helping them expand – globally if they want. That sounds like something you'd be proud to be a part of, whatever your job.

Questions to Ponder

What are our current propositions? What are we transforming for whom? Why do they care? (The purpose of the transformation).

Can we express our core proposition in 7-12 words?

What about 3 words? Let's go further. Is there a *single* word that encapsulates the transformation you bring?

How clearly do people across our business and its various roles see propositions? Do people connect with the transformations customers will experience?

Are our offerings and propositions consistent and congruent with our customers and budget? For example, are we pitching a budget experience at a premium price, or underselling a valuable transformation at too low a perceived price to be credible?

What do staff across the business think we do for customers? Do they see our offerings in terms of being a transformation? Or are customers just a necessary evil between pay packets? (What might change that if so?)

Do our propositions fit with our business's longer term goals? Are we promising transformations to customers that fit with the overall purpose of the business? For example, are our propositions about getting quick results, but we've shifted our business purpose to focus on the quality of long-term outcomes? Are these two goals achievable with our current ways of working?

Your Notes And Contemplations

- What has come out of your musings on these areas?
- What questions have been raised in your mind about fit with the organisation's purpose?
- What facts can you note down (what's your evidence)?
- What assumptions can you validate with your team, peers or colleagues?
- What do you feel you need to understand (analyse) better?
- What do you feel compelled to fix or address? Why?

Part Two – The Preparation

Products & Services – Delivery

Introduction

With all the previous talk of "desire and trust" and the promises of transformation in our propositions, I'm sure you'll be thinking "ah yes, but then we've got to make it all happen!"

And yes, how true that is. It's probably what your paying customers care most about. You know, getting what they believe they paid for...

So, we have seen that the proposition is about engaging customers and inspiring our staff. When it comes to The Flow of Purpose, delivery is about people taking the responsibility to take the action, and produce the things, which in turn create those wonderful, meaningful transformations for our customers.

Purposeful delivery tends to need communication and clarity. It is often about having clearly communicated requirements; expected results or outcomes. Clarity about priorities and timing of work can affect perceptions of delivery. The perceived quality of delivery links closely with purpose – why are we delivering in a certain way, for example? To make our lives easy, control costs, deliver highest quality, reduce delivery time, or something else? Will the client see it the same way?

There's also a fundamental need to make sure that people know what they're supposed to be doing as part of delivering outcomes. So obvious, yet how many times have I seen staff pretty much left to their own devices? Working in ways which are governed by a mixture of historic forms, cobbled together checklists, and corporate folklore passed down through the generations of workers.

Our customers want to buy things from us for a reason (whether services or products). Whilst they wait for the outcomes of our work, they are still driven by their purpose – the big why that drove them to trust us, and buy from us. We could conclude then, that purposeful delivery also means keeping customers informed of how we are doing in meeting their purpose. How are we doing at removing or reducing the pain that compelled them to buy from us? How are we working towards delighting them? On the flip side, how are they working with us – do we see the same purpose as we did at the start, or are different agendas starting to muddy the waters? Do their accountable people know about any "drift" of purpose?

Communicating well through delivery (especially linked to the purpose of the purchase) also means we stand more of a chance of spotting any expectations that have gone a bit awry.

Whether we're selling a one-dollar pen or a multi-million-pound ERP project, there is always value in reviewing whether the delivered offering actually met the intended purpose. Of course, for a dollar pen, the cost of getting feedback on its fit to purpose might not be cost-effective. It's probably worth your while finding out how your multi-million-pound project was perceived though...

OK, I know, in this latter case, it sounds obvious – duh, of course we get feedback on something that big! However, unless a strong core purpose has been carefully nurtured through the whole procurement and delivery process, we could find that different stakeholders wanted different transformations. They saw the purpose of the project from a different viewpoint. It's surprising – my experience has been that you don't need that big a project, sale or transformation to start to see these "cross-purposes" popping up.

Questions of purpose also raise their heads for the delivery of ongoing services. For example, you and your team might offer a weekly social media content service to customers. Multiple "whys" are at play here. There's the proposition you promised to deliver to the customer – the promise of transformation that they bought. There's the impact you want the revenue and commitment to have on the growth and performance of your business. There's the opportunity to grow people so that they create more value. I'm sure that you can think of many more whys – types of purpose – for services, that would apply to your business.

Especially when we find ourselves driven by metrics and KPIs, there is a risk that the true purpose of day-to-day work can get lost. We need to always feel that we provide our service diligently, to meet both our and our customers' purposes. We need to call out inconsistencies or divergence if we are to always feel our work is relevant and valuable.

Questions to Ponder

Are our delivery processes defined? Do people understand the purpose of each step in the process? Why we do things the way we do?

Do people know where their role fits into the overall delivery process? Do they know what good looks like? Do they know why customers rely on us so much?

How do we give appropriate people authority to intervene in delivery and make "human decisions" to meet customer purpose better? How do we track this, so that we can spot patterns and make systemic improvements?

What responsibilities do customers have? How do they know that?

How do we define, communicate, refine and share our ways of working? How do staff engage with them to make them better? Do they feel they have a say? Do they? Who listens to them? Who has the authority to decide on change?

What systems or processes do we have in place to ensure quality delivery? We're looking for the checks and balances that protect us from "people having a bad day" turning into letting customers down.

Do we use a CRM system or similar way of having one view of the truth and what transformation we are delivering to each of our customers?

Your Notes And Contemplations

- What has come out of your musings on these areas?
- What questions have been raised in your mind about fit with the organisation's purpose?
- What facts can you note down (what's your evidence)?
- What assumptions can you validate with your team, peers or colleagues?
- What do you feel you need to understand (analyse) better?
- What do you feel compelled to fix or address? Why?

Part Two – The Preparation

Products & Services – Innovation

Introduction

Like so many aspects of what I do around purpose and process, a great many brilliant minds know and put things better than I ever could, when it comes to innovation.

By its nature, I suppose, attitudes and approaches to innovation are always changing. There are a stream of new books, blog posts, LinkedIn articles and the like, telling us how we should be innovating nowadays.

Peter Drucker is often regarded as one of the most influential thinkers on management in modern times. In an article for the Harvard Business Review in 2002[5], Drucker wrote (with my emphasis in bold):

> *"Innovation is the specific function of entrepreneurship, whether in an existing business, a public service institution, or a new venture started by a lone individual in the family kitchen. It is the means by which the entrepreneur either creates new wealth-producing resources or endows existing resources with enhanced potential for creating wealth.*
>
> *Today, much confusion exists about the proper definition of entrepreneurship. Some observers use the term to refer to all small businesses; others, to all new businesses. In practice, however, a great many well-established businesses engage in highly successful entrepreneurship. The term, then, refers not to an enterprise's size or age but to a certain kind of activity. At the heart of that activity is innovation: the effort to* **create purposeful, focused change** *in an enterprise's economic or social potential.*
>
> <u>Sources of Innovation</u>
>
> *There are, of course, innovations that spring from a flash of genius. Most innovations, however, especially the successful ones, result from a* **conscious, purposeful search** *for innovation opportunities, which are found only in a few*

---

[5] https://hbr.org/2002/08/the-discipline-of-innovation

> situations. Four such areas of opportunity exist within a company or industry: unexpected occurrences, incongruities, process needs, and industry and market changes.
>
> Three additional sources of opportunity exist outside a company in its social and intellectual environment: demographic changes, changes in perception, and new knowledge...
>
> ...**Purposeful, systematic innovation** begins with the **analysis** of the sources of new opportunities...
>
> ...Because innovation is both conceptual and perceptual, would-be innovators must also go out and look, ask, and listen. Successful innovators use both the right and left sides of their brains. They work out analytically what the innovation **has to be** to satisfy an opportunity. Then they go out and look at **potential users to study their expectations, their values, and their needs.**"

To Drucker, the most successful way of innovating, is to be purposeful in meeting users' needs. That sounds a lot like a flow of purpose.

Paraphrasing quite a bit, Peter Drucker also said that for businesses, only marketing and innovation are investments, everything else is a cost.

Bluntly put, innovation is what gives your customers new things to buy, or reasons to buy from you rather than competitors.

This is interesting from a Flow of Purpose standpoint. The implication is that innovation should be matched by some sort of shift in purpose – or that a shift in purpose may need to be met through innovation.

It's not always the case that we need to innovate because the customer shifts their purpose. However, it's quite intriguing to think about what we might do if we track changes in purpose, the "new whys," that our customers share with us. Might these be opportunities to grow, adapt and innovate what we offer to customers? New things to buy? New reasons to buy from us?

By extension then, how do we stay close to our customers to spot changes in their purpose?

How do we excite our customers about changes in our purpose – and what that could mean for their businesses?

There are all sorts of ways of approaching innovation in organisations. Let me share some of the things that I've seen work over the years.

- Internal incubators
- Market research and pitching ideas
- Innovation workshops or events
- Focused sabbaticals to create minimum viable products
- Joint working with clients
- Working with external consultants or designers
- Looking at precedents for innovation in "adjacent" industries
- Innovation groups, guilds or teams.

The most important thing, is that our *purpose* now and in the future should be front and centre of what we create. The exciting new "what and how" should not compromise the "why" – though "what and how" may strengthen "why" if we get innovation right.

There is an extraordinary amount of information out there in books, on the web and in courses and guides on innovation. You won't run short of stimulation and education! This is one of those areas where you'll need to make a judgement call on what will work in your business or organisation.

Be innovative!

Questions to Ponder

Does our organisation identify and value innovation as necessary – does it feel like innovation has a clear business purpose, or is it an ad-hoc activity? (Or even accidental?)

Who's responsible for innovation in your organisation? How well do they do? How well are they supported?

How much time and effort would we estimate is spent on Innovation? How do we think that compares with (especially) marketing? Why might this ratio be as it is?

What might happen if we innovated more? Less?

If "more" – would we end up with more new products or waste more time on more ideas? If "Less" – would we have better focus on winning ideas, or insufficient time to produce proper minimum viable products?

What drives our innovation? New things we can do, market trends, or things our customers are crying out for?

Do we have an outline process for innovating, so we can understand what works for our organisation?

How do we measure the success of innovation?

Would third party involvement help our innovation? If so, how?

Your Notes And Contemplations

- What has come out of your musings on these areas?
- What questions have been raised in your mind about fit with the organisation's purpose?
- What facts can you note down (what's your evidence)?
- What assumptions can you validate with your team, peers or colleagues?
- What do you feel you need to understand (analyse) better?
- What do you feel compelled to fix or address? Why?

10 Exploring Profit

Our core philosophy here is:

People need to feel accountable for the costs and value they create for the business and buyers.

Profit – Income & Value

Introduction

When analysing purpose, income is what we get as an appropriate financial reward for the promises we fulfil to our customers. There are many steps and responsibilities in the chain that leads to us getting paid or receiving income. For a flow of purpose, each one of us needs to understand why and how our role can affect our income.

That implies we need to dig into a few different things. These include the levels of value, pricing and income we actually receive.

We need to examine if we always get paid for valuable offerings – or if we consciously choose not to, what reciprocation do we get in return? We might give something valuable away to secure access to someone, or make them warmer towards our main proposition.

We might look at why our income is structured in the way it is.

Quality, in particular perceived quality, is an important aspect to consider too, as it is often one of the ways we can use to check if our offerings are delivering what we promised when we sold them.

If what we deliver is seen as a valuable contributor to a client's purpose, then they will be willing to pay us more than if our service does little to support their purpose. We need to be an important part of the difference they make in the world. If we understand their purpose and it aligns with ours – then we create value and boost income.

Questions to Ponder

How do people know what impact their work has on the income we can expect from customers?

Will faster results, higher quality, clearer value or something else mean that customers are happy to pay, and pay more? How is that explained in our training, processes or documentation?

How do our people feel when they know, or find out, that we haven't delivered value, especially if that means customers don't want to pay us on time, in full? Are there signs that failing in our purpose creates a pain that our people want to remedy? How much do people care when things go wrong? How can we leverage this to improve how we work?

If we put our prices up, would customers still see our offering as good value? If we put our prices down, could we sell more? What parts are there in this equation?

How do customers pay us? In advance? In arrears? Staged? Subscription? Why did we choose these ways of paying, and are they still relevant?

What can we do with our processes and people management to help underline to our teams that each of our work adds to (or detracts from) the value a customer gets from us?

If our organisation is a charity or not for profit, how do we get our income; grants, donations, selling offerings, etc? What do we need to do to show the value that these income streams create? How does that affect our processes?

Can we introduce new income streams? Are there things we can do, supply or explain that are valuable to customers?

How involved and motivated do different people and roles across our business feel in creating and delivering value? What great ideas are there to be captured and used?

How will we recognise people who come up with and implement ideas that create value?

Your Notes And Contemplations

- What has come out of your musings on these areas?
- What questions have been raised in your mind about fit with the organisation's purpose?
- What facts can you note down (what's your evidence)?
- What assumptions can you validate with your team, peers or colleagues?
- What do you feel you need to understand (analyse) better?
- What do you feel compelled to fix or address? Why?

Profit – Costs

Introduction

Costs are necessary in running an organisation. Unnecessary costs are horribly painful, because they are "on the bottom line". Costs: once you've got one, there's nothing you can do about it...

When I was a technical manager, I used to explain it to my team of engineers like this:

- Let's say our business makes a net profit of 10% after we've paid all the things we need to (keeps the maths easy!).
- That gives us £100 of money to use as we wish for every £1000 engineer day we sell (i.e. £100 is 10% of our £1000 turnover).
- Conversely, if we want to spend £100 we hadn't bargained for, to cover that cost, we'll need to sell an *extra* £1000 day.
- What if we need to do 2 days of remedial or extra work because we made a mistake or got our statement of work wrong?

- Let's assume an engineer day costs us about £400 with all of the salary, expenses, etc. factored in.
- So, our extra cost is £800 for 2 days.
- But... this is extra cost, so if we are not to affect our profit at the end of the year, we'll need to sell more to cover that £800.
- In fact, we need to sell £8,000 extra if our net profit is 10% - i.e. an £8,000 sale gets us the extra £800 we now need.
- So that mistake in spec or delivery ultimately needed 8 days more to be sold on top of current targets.

"That," I would say, "is why we need to really focus on accuracy and costs..."

Of course, this example is over-simplified in accounting terms, but it does help to make the point.

Focusing on costs is not necessarily about being miserly or cutting, cutting, cutting.

It *is* about saying "does this cost help us deliver our purpose, does it help our customer deliver their purpose?"

Many, many books, courses and experts are out there on the mechanics of costs – fixed costs, variable costs, direct costs, indirect costs, costs of sale, costs of doing business. The list goes on.

There are costs that can be measured in financial terms, there are time costs (delays, excess effort), and there are reputational costs associated with decisions, action or inaction.

For The Flow of Purpose, what we are most interested in is "why would we accept this cost? What does it allow us to do?"

Questions to Ponder

How clearly known are costs in our organisation? Is it consistent across departments and teams?

Have we done any work to figure out where & how we accrue costs?

Who is accountable for what parts of our cost base? Do they have a clear purpose to why they are spending on costs – how do purchases or spends enable purpose?

How much do individuals identify with being responsible for their own costs? How do or could we help people be clear on costs associated with their roles?

What could we do to spot, manage and avoid excess costs?

Are some things seen as costs when they should be seen as investments? Vice versa? Who is involved in these decisions? How can we change their view of why we are/should be spending?

Your Notes And Contemplations

- What has come out of your musings on these areas?
- What questions have been raised in your mind about fit with the organisation's purpose?
- What facts can you note down (what's your evidence)?
- What assumptions can you validate with your team, peers or colleagues?
- What do you feel you need to understand (analyse) better?
- What do you feel compelled to fix or address? Why?

Part Three – The Practicalities

Part Three – The Practicalities

Part Three – The Practicalities

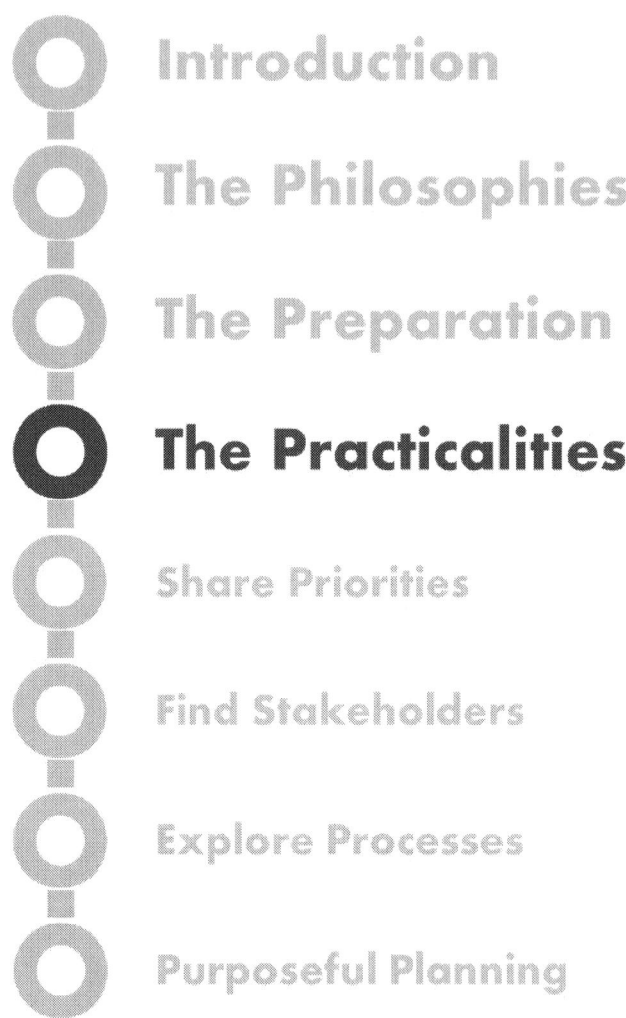

Part Three – The Practicalities

11 The Flow of Purpose – Making It Happen

In Part Three, I'm going to share with you the simple yet powerful tools that I use with my clients. They are tools that bring people together to set and share vision, encourage debate and discussion, explore purpose and needs, and analyse our situation and options.

The tools are predominantly diagrams which individuals and groups can use to stimulate, contain, explore and document discussions and decisions. They are a start point for you to build upon and adapt.

When we use them alongside a clear purpose, we drive improvements and innovation through our organisations, because people understand why we must change and what a difference change will make.

For each of the diagrams, I'll walk you through how it fits with The Flow of Purpose, how it works, what outcomes you can expect, and some of the ways you can get the most out of it.

Before we work through the tools, let's start by making sure that your organisation's purpose is clear.

Part Three – The Practicalities

12 Set Your Purpose & Strategy

What is "Purpose" Anyway?

At the start of the book, I shared my dictionary's definition of purpose:

Purpose n. reason for which something is done or exists; determination; practical advantage or use.

What would your definition of purpose be? Not "what is *your* purpose?", but "what *is* purpose, as a concept?"

For example, once when I was asked to define purpose, I wrote this:

Purpose is the driving force behind taking action, not taking action, or making one decision over another; in order to make a difference that matters to those I care about.

We need to get to a situation where our business, and often the people and teams in it, have their definition of what purpose *means*, so that we can say with clarity what our purpose *is*.

Does that make sense?

If we're clear on the concept, and what it encompasses, we'll get a more compelling purpose.

Part Three – The Practicalities

In turn, a more compelling purpose will be more meaningful, to more people across our organisation.

It will drive better outcomes.

It is worth investing time on purpose before anything else, even if it feels like it is unnecessary, overkill, or too difficult to get people agreeing.

Our organisation's purpose has to be shared by everyone, so often, creating it is a group exercise. That said, you can still follow the process on your own, if you need to be more direct or proactive.

How Shall We State Our Purpose?

I suggest setting up a "Statement of Purpose Meeting" with your leadership group to have them:

- create definitions of purpose,
- agree a joint definition,
- create fragments of a statement of purpose, and then
- agree a joint statement of purpose.

If we have a definition, and we know our situation, we can write a great purpose.

Figure 4 What Purpose means in our context

If you have a small leadership group, who are already well aligned, creating a great statement of purpose might take an hour.

If you have a more disparate, less aligned, less communicative or congruent leadership group, it could take days just to explore and agree a statement of purpose. It may even take days or weeks of cajoling just to get people to agree it is necessary or valuable.

What if people won't play ball?

There are many reasons why this can be the case; growth, personality clashes, work overload or many other things. Stick with it though. Sometimes asking people to consider the opposite scenario can help convince people to take part. You could ask your leaders and thinkers "can we ever be at our best if everyone is working to a different vision, for different reasons?"

You may also have picked up that I wrote "leadership group" rather than "management team". The leaders in your organisation may not be solely in management roles. Subject matter experts, team leaders, entrepreneurial thinkers and experienced, grizzled old hands may all have something to offer in leading thinking.

You may want to take some time to consider who is in your leadership group? Is that who you'd naturally invite to a purpose session? Think broadly and creatively!

A final thought – who is accountable for purpose in your organisation?

Ideally the accountability should rest at the very top – MD, CEO or chairperson.

What if you have taken on responsibility to introduce The Flow of Purpose, but don't head up your organisation? My suggestion would be to find the person who is (or who you think should be) accountable for purpose, and get them onside, fast. They may be up for it, or they may take some convincing that it is their responsibility and that work is needed. If they believe in The Flow of Purpose before you start working, life will be a whole lot easier with their backing. Otherwise the risk is that people may accuse you of trying hijack or force through some new purpose for your own agenda. This can all be managed with dialogue, but can feel like wading through treacle.

Part Three – The Practicalities

Running a Statement of Purpose Meeting

Let's assume you are ready to work on the first step – writing a statement of purpose, by calling a meeting of the leaders and thinkers.

I suggest starting your agenda by stating and writing up the objective of the session (e.g. "to define purpose for our organisation") as this is consistent with what we want to achieve – the start of The Flow of Purpose. As an aside, when we use The Flow of Purpose diagrams, we start with the purpose as the first item on the board. So, starting the statement of purpose meeting with the objective is congruent with this approach. Every discussion, every decision, every action must be working towards that objective; they must be purposeful.

Next, ask each person to state or write a definition of "purpose" – remember, at this stage we want people to think about what might be written in a dictionary, not what your organisation's purpose is. What we're doing here is getting people to think about why a clear purpose matters, by breaking the concept down.

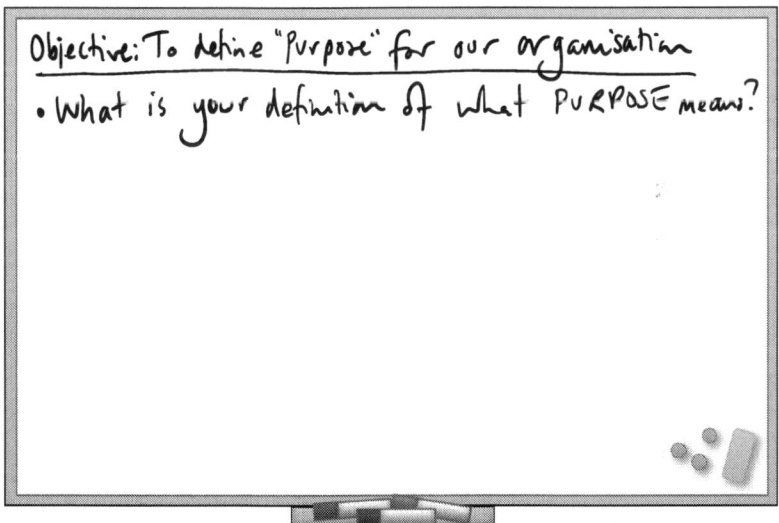

Figure 5 Start sessions with an objective or purpose

Get people to share their definitions of purpose and promote discussion. Ideally, write the definitions up on a screen, flipchart or whiteboard. We

Part Three – The Practicalities

want constructive debate on key aspects that are common or different across people's definitions. We're looking to spot clues for where different roles or personalities might clash or complement one another, even at this stage.

Working through the potential definitions of "purpose" as a group can often show subtle differences in our drivers compared to others. Since we all chose to work in the same organisation, it's likely that we think along roughly the same lines. However differences of emphasis that we see now, may be magnified when our purpose starts to push further out into the organisation.

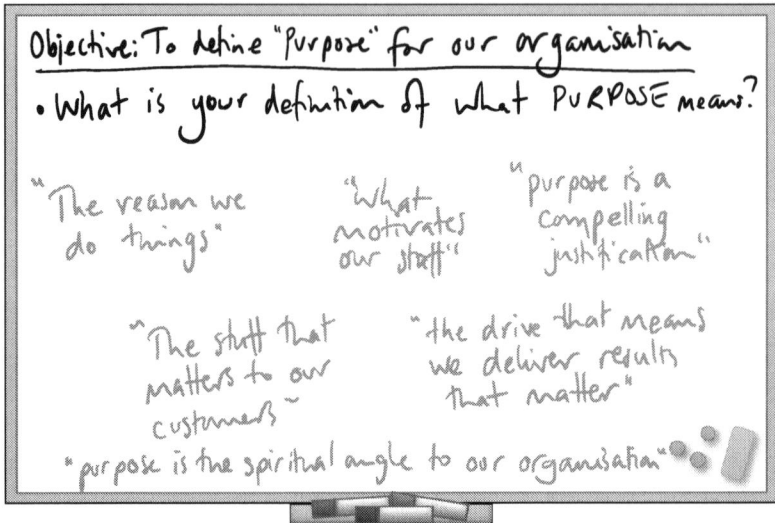

Figure 6 Collect ideas to look for themes & differences

Work together to debate, argue, vote on or otherwise decide on a single definition for what purpose means. What we have now are the component parts that, as a group, we think are needed to make a statement of purpose.

When you have your agreed definition, write it up on the board.

Let's say you've taken your notes like the example above, and turned them into your own, single definition of what "purpose" *means*.

Next, we need to agree what our purpose *is*.

Here, I suggest not trying to write a statement or sentence to begin with – maybe not even in this session. What is more important is coming up with, and discussing, the sentiments, words and fragments that properly express the intent of the purpose. Crafting the perfect sentence can come later if needed. You have your definition of what the word "purpose" *means*. Lots of sources could feed into what your organisation's purpose actually *is*.

You may have a mission statement, or a statement of your core values. Your branding may convey certain values. Often though, the "why" behind these values is not always clear, especially the further away in the organisation chart you get from the group that wrote them...

Note: If you want to test this idea, get everyone in the meeting to start with your organisation's mission statement, vision or values, and ask them to write the compelling "why" beside each word, phrase or sentence. Does everyone write the same things? In most organisations, I'd be willing to bet not. This is the difference between "purpose" and "vision" or "values" – the sense of "why", or "because". Vision is "what?", purpose answers "so what?"

There may be marketplace or compliance pressures that you know you need to take into account within your purpose. For example, you might suggest some words saying "we make sure we stay compliant with health & safety law to protect our people."

Consider that definition I wrote earlier in the chapter: "Purpose is the driving force behind taking action, not taking action, or making one decision over another; in order to make a difference that matters to those I care about."

If I was using this as our start point for our meeting, I'd be looking at prompting discussion with questions like:

- What driving force is behind our work? Who cares about what?
- What difference do we make, to whom?
- What sort of action do we take (that our customer wouldn't, hence needing us)?
- How do we conduct ourselves when taking action? What does that mean for our staff and customers?
- Why might we not take action? What boundaries do we have in place? Why? Are the reasons for boundaries ethical, financial, legal or people-related?
- What do we prioritise when we decide? What are our rules for prioritising? Why have they become our rules? Do we feel our staff

and customers would recognise these rules when we make our decisions?
- Why does anyone care about the difference we seek to make? Are we removing pain, enabling opportunity or creating delight or distraction? Why does what we do matter?
- What is it that makes us care about certain people? Is it our social mission? Is it because they pay us money? Do they bring us repeat business? Do they influence others? Is it just plain ol' good manners?

A great way to run this sort of session is to break your definition down into blocks on a whiteboard, and then mind-map the comments, answers and questions.

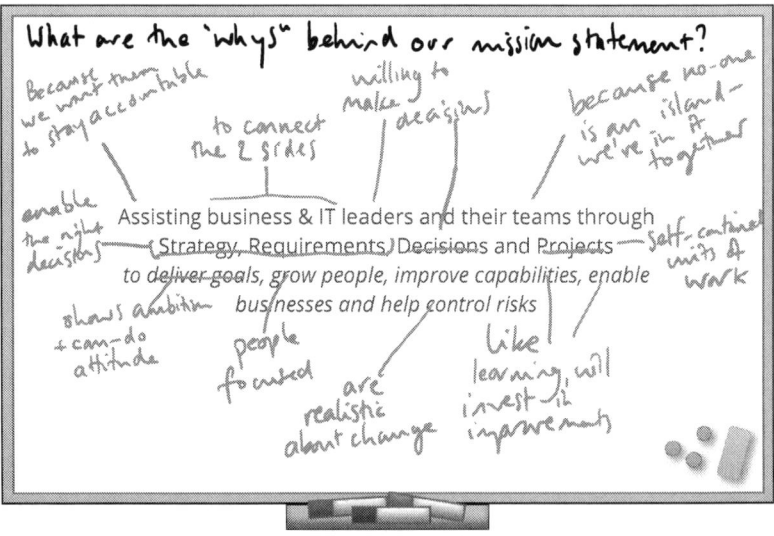

Figure 7 An example of exploring a mission statement for purpose

That gets everything "out there" to be seen. This is often enough to prompt constructive debate on what should be in the organisation's purpose.

Normally, there will be at least a couple of sticky points that we find difficult to get immediate consensus on.

There are a few approaches you can use to unlock these sorts of situations.

You can "take them offline" – in other words, give everyone a day or two to mull things over and come back to the question. If you do this, be aware that

Part Three – The Practicalities

momentum can seep away when people leave the room. Maybe set up a follow-on meeting, explicitly to resolve the offline items, agreed by everyone whilst they are in the room.

You can have the accountable person make a decision, explaining why. If this feels like a loose end type of approach, you can always say that the decision is a "key working assumption" rather than a final decision. With this approach, that leaves the door open to making a change if new facts come to light that prove or disprove the assumption.

Giving people "votes" can work well if there are semantic or circular arguments going on. You can do this with paper sticky-dots, pen-marks on the white board, or a simple show of hands. My preferred route is the show of hands, with each person getting, e.g. 3 or 4 votes to cast. I go round the table, each person getting one vote at a time. I ask them where their vote is going, and why they have chosen it. They can vote for the same thing multiple times, but only on successive rounds. This forces people to think of priority.

The last stage to go through is crafting a readable, and believable statement of purpose that aims to include your highest priority words and phrases. This might take a few iterations.

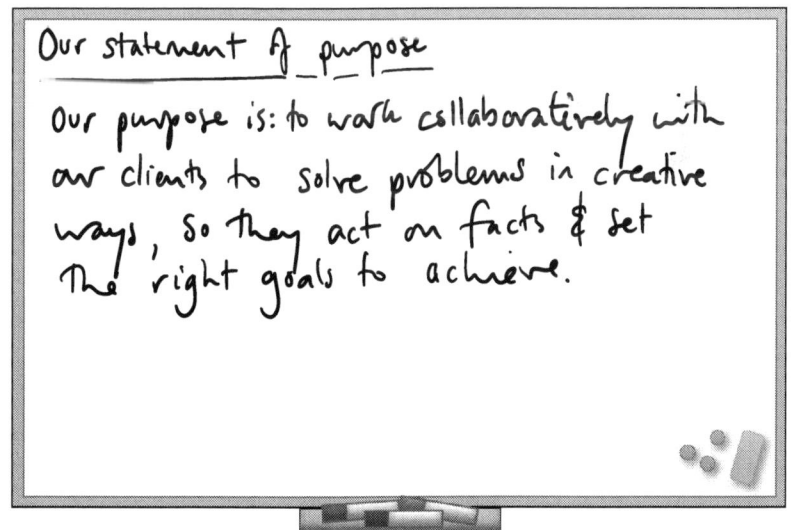

Figure 8 An example of an initial statement of purpose

What we need to produce ultimately is a statement that we could imagine anyone in the business reading or saying out loud, feeling that it was relevant to their role, and making them feel they make a difference. (The statement should still fit our definition for "purpose").

To recap, here is my suggested agenda for an initial Statement of Purpose Meeting. Feel free to modify it.

Agenda:

- Review and agree the meeting objective: "to define purpose for our organisation"
- Define what we mean by "purpose"
- Brainstorm around our purpose
- Agree our outline/initial purpose elements
- Craft our Statement of Purpose.

More Analysis Resources For You

I mentioned at the start of this section that a clear purpose comes from a shared definition and an understanding of your situation.

We've already covered a fair bit of how to create a definition for "purpose", but what if you find people are struggling with gaining a clear understanding of our situation? This can happen after periods of rapid growth, organisational change, mergers/acquisitions or market developments.

I'd like to share with you some ideas to help explore your situation.

Gap Analysis

The first is the good old "gap analysis". A gap analysis is simply two descriptions – one of where we are now, and one for where we want to be – and a list of the differences between the two descriptions. It tells us the gap we have from now to our desired future. If we know the gaps, then we can investigate and address them.

Gap analyses can be very simple, or they can be very detailed and complex documents. As you can imagine, for our purposes here, we want the simple end of the spectrum.

Start by thinking, as a group, about what you do as a business, for whom and why. (Ideally do this "situation" work after you have your definition for purpose). Write them down as your "parameters".

Grab a handy whiteboard and draw up two big blobs, one on the left (now) and one on the right (future).

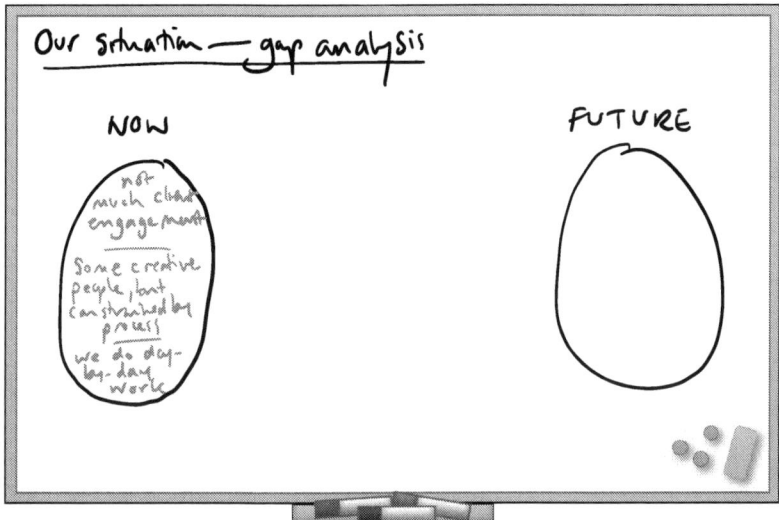

Figure 9 An example current state in a gap analysis

In the left blob, write a set of short statements that reflect how well you do these things now. Don't sweat the details.

Next, write a matching set of short statements in the right blob for how you should be doing these things in future. If you can, include a "why" – why do you want the future to be different?

Are there any extra things you want to be doing in the future that have no equivalent "in the now"? If so, write them in on the right hand side, and make a note on the left hand side that we don't yet do these things.

Part Three – The Practicalities

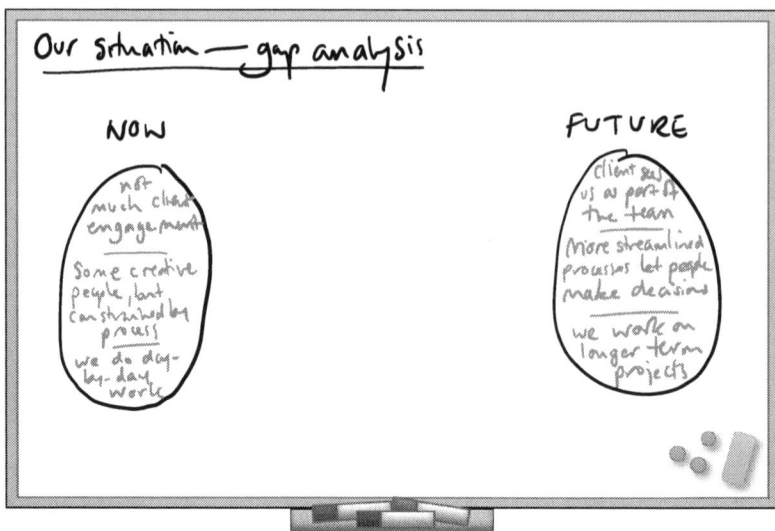

Figure 10 Adding future state ideas to the gap analysis

Now, brainstorm and write up in the gap between the two blobs what is missing between the two blobs, for each entry. What do we need to start, stop or change with what we do? Why? Write these "steps to the future" down.

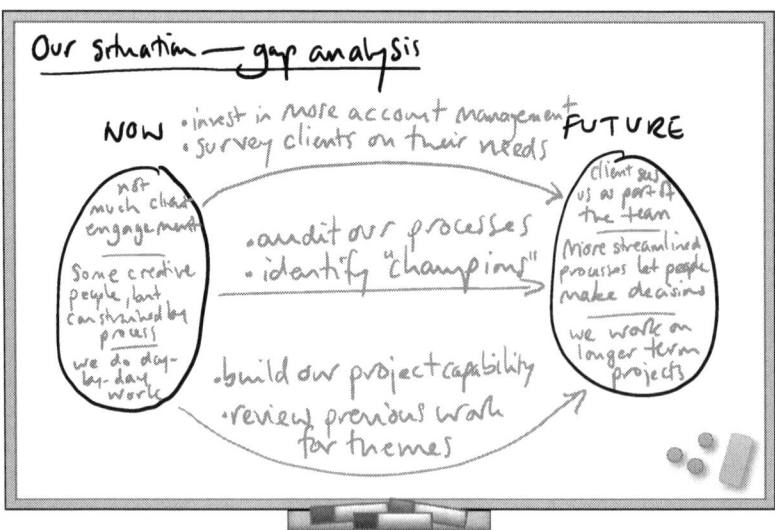

Figure 11 Stimulating ideas for purpose by looking at now -> future

Compare the steps and their whys to your definition of purpose.

How would they fit together to create a statement of purpose? Do they illuminate our thinking? Raise new questions?

The Nine Word Business Model

If you like the idea of the gap analysis, but are finding the tricky bit is in defining the now and the future, you can use my Nine Word Business Model to assemble your group's thoughts.

Over the course of my career, I've tried to boil down the why, what and how of doing business to a minimal set of key words. They are designed to be a set of broad headings that can be used for documents, discussions, debates and so on. They also help us to compare different ideas or options, by considering our options from each of the nine keywords.

I've grouped the nine words into three areas. Let me share them, and then explain how I think they might help you.

Area	Key Words		
Commercial Imperative	Profitability	Risk	Differentiation
Our Assets	People	Process	Technology
Getting It Done	Ownership	Communication	Priority

Commercial Imperative

Commercial Imperative means the reasons why we would invest time and money in creating or changing something. In order for work to be meaningful, it should improve at least one of profitability, risk or differentiation.

Profitability. It could be that the thing you intend to do (project, training, new development, etc.) helps you reduce the cost of something, or increase the income from something. Both of these would help profitability. They create a sense of imperative, a sense of need.

Risk. Risks are the situations that we don't yet know the outcome of. We're not sure they'll happen, and we don't fully know what impact they'll have. That doesn't mean we should ignore them. When thinking about purpose and our gap analysis, what ideas can we come up with for how we get better information, faster, so fewer things are unknown? What ideas are there for making it easier for us to deal with the unexpected if it does happen?

Differentiation. The reasons customers buy from us, rather than other suppliers. Is it part of our purpose to help customers be differentiated too? What do we do now to support being differentiated? What would help us stand out better in future?

Our Assets

Our assets are the valuable things we have that help us operate our organisation.

People. Our people are not just "headcount" – in the nine word model, people means the effort available to us, skills that people have, their motivation, "churn" and a host of other things. When you are discussing purpose and current/future states, look to discuss these types of aspect of your people. What will be different in future? Why?

Process. To be valuable to your business, your processes should be defined and available in such a way that if most of the people changed, you would still run in the same way, giving customers the same results they have come to expect, given the same requirements and "inputs". Can you say that about your processes now? Are they dependent on some key individuals – would you even know if they are, unless that key person leaves? And how do your processes work in general now? How would you like your processes to be in future?

Technology. These are the tools that help us be productive, efficient, consistent and accurate. Tools are everything from pens and paper forms, to enterprise-wide online systems that automate hundreds of tasks. How does your technology serve you now? What would it need to do for you and your customers in future? Why is that advancement or change important – how does it affect purpose?

Getting It Done

Our commercial imperative gives us our reasons to change, and our assets are the things we change – this section is how we ensure that change happens. You could call it things like change management, project management, continuous improvement, or accountability. I prefer the simpler name of "Getting It Done".

Part Three – The Practicalities

Ownership. Most people are used to putting initials next to actions (hopefully along with a date to be done by). That's not quite the same as ownership. Ownership is more of a hearts and minds thing. We're looking to have people who care about delivering the things they have ownership of. Pride in the work and the difference it makes. Think of ownership as "responsibility with purpose". Or "caring"... For the gap analysis, perhaps ask: How well do we own things right now? How do we show people the difference their ownership makes? How could ownership be different in future? What information, skills and systems might support that?

Communication. Ah, perhaps the most vital word in operating a business... Over the years, when I've done post-mortems of projects which have either gone well or badly, there are usually two root causes – communication or prioritisation. We either communicated or prioritised well; or we got the communication or the prioritisation wrong. And essentially, prioritisation is a form of communication! What we don't want to do though is over-communicate. This is as much of a problem as under- or mis-communication. Who here feels they don't get enough email, and don't get to go to enough meetings? What's an appropriate level or type of communication to meet your purpose? How is your approach working now? Is there anything you'd change, driven by your definition of purpose?

Priority. Priority is one of my personal fascinations and bugbears in equal part. Priority, to me, means doing the right thing first. In fact, I believe that there was no plural for priority until the 19th or 20th century, when it became possible to have "priori*ties*" – many most important things at once! The Industrial Revolution has a lot to answer for.

Yes, prioritisation can be really difficult. However, it's my contention that it's more important to manage priority than time.

Properly manage priority and time will manage itself (to a point, of course).

Managing time can completely miss priorities.

Another pet peeve of mine: "Management" hand down a list of strategic priorities to their staff – the big stuff we need to change about our business. Management also hand down a list of operational priorities – how our day to day activities rank relative to one another. Management almost never hands down a single list of priorities that encompasses both strategic and operational priorities.

Part Three – The Practicalities

Think of it this way; is it fair to give the workers at the sharp end two separate priority lists and ask them to resolve them, whilst they have customers in front of them, and then beat your staff up when they don't deliver the strategic changes? Or, have a go at them when they do the exciting strategic stuff and ignore the customers that pay the bills?

I have asked senior management teams to take their strategic and operational priorities, and put them in one list. And, I've been told more than once "that would be too difficult and time-consuming to do".

Riiight... Let's just think about that for a minute... It's too difficult for the brightest brains in the business to properly judge their own competing priorities, but we expect our junior staff to ace it every day.

Hmm. How much better if we helped our management teams and staff by sharing our view of how strategy and serving customers fit together – even if we're just giving a suggested split of effort in percentage terms?

So, given my priority-based ranting here, could you deliver better on your organisation's purpose if you changed things in future? How might prioritisation fit with your definition of purpose?

Could you, as a leadership group, come up with a single view of operational and strategic priorities? I guarantee you that it will create debate if you do.

Go on – I dare you!

I've even drawn you a diagram to get you started... You could draw up your two lists in priority order (debates 1 and 2) and then work out how you share a single list across your staff (debate 3).

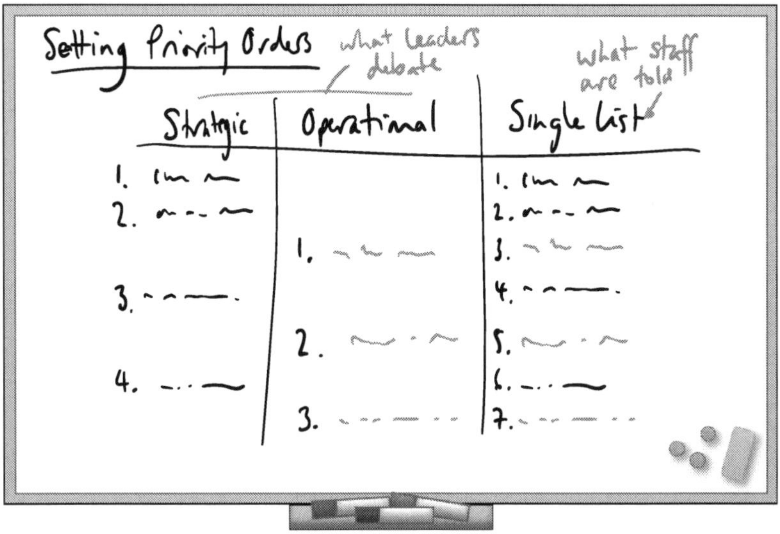

Part Three – The Practicalities

Figure 12 A rant about having one list of priorities

Using The Nine Words With The Gap Analysis

The Nine Word Business Model is a broader tool I use across my consulting, but I felt it would be useful to share in the context of discussing your current and future states, the gap between them, and your purpose overall. You don't need to use my nine words – you may well have all the input and ideas you need from your group participants – great!

By this point, possibly through using a gap analysis and the Nine Word Business Model, you should have a statement of purpose for your business. It's the foundation for working with The Flow of Purpose.

Now, we are ready to start using your purpose to explore, discuss, document and improve the way your organisation operates. We are ready to show how purpose can bring your people together to deliver the things that matter to your customers.

Part Three – The Practicalities

13 Let Your Purpose Flow

On your marks... Get set...

I wanted to find a way to make the analysis work that I was doing matter more to people and to organisations. I wanted to find a way of making sure that the insight I helped generate, the diagrams I drew and the designs and reports I created didn't just end up gathering dust.

As we've read, purpose is a powerful thing – lots of clever thinkers, writers and bloggers have shared incredible, inspiring and compelling reasons for this.

I wondered if purpose might be the answer to making my work matter more. A sense of "why". A "because" that people believed in.

I figured that if people really "got" the *why* behind the work, they would be more willing to value it. They might even be interested in getting involved with it. They might even look forward to implementing the changes that result from analysis and design work. Imagine that, people who want changes to ways of working to succeed!

Robert Cialdini et al performed an interesting experiment with a photocopier, which they documented in their book "Yes! 50 secrets from the science of persuasion". I encourage you to read the story. Actually, the whole

Part Three – The Practicalities

book[6]. Anyway, I won't spoil the detail for you, but the conclusion was that the word "because" has tremendous power. If you say you are doing something *for a purpose*, people are much, much more likely to buy in and help you.

So, The Flow of Purpose is about always knowing our "because". For example, here are the "becauses" (in grey) for why we move through each tool/stage:

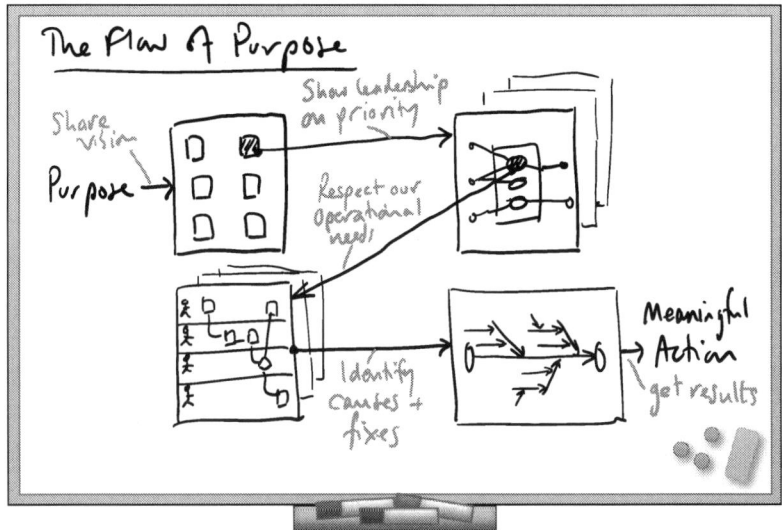

Figure 13 The Flow of Purpose through the four diagrams

Making purpose flow is largely about building a habit of making sure that, whenever we do something, we have a clear "because" for it. Not just any because. A "because" which links right back to our organisation's overarching purpose. A "why" that is explained by our statement of purpose. That keeps everyone working towards the same ends, for the same reasons.

Each of the analysis tools we use in The Flow of Purpose has, as a first step, a reminder of our statement of purpose. To that we add the outcome we want from the step, and the "because" for the piece of work.

---

[6] "Yes! : 50 Secrets From the Science of Persuasion", Professor R Cialdini , N Goldstein , S Martin, Profile Books Ltd

Getting People to Believe in Purpose

Splendid. All very well. We can show how individual bits of work have a place in our overall purpose. We may well feel totally fired up about this new sense of purpose. We can see how it will help us change our organisation for the better.

But if purpose is to truly flow through our business, we still need to bring our staff along with us:

- Our driven senior management
- Our busy middle management
- Our delivery focused team leaders
- Our busy colleagues with varying levels of current engagement.

We need people to buy in to our purpose, whoever they are.

If you've read Part Two of The Flow of Purpose, you may recall me talking about "Desire and Trust". I talked through how buyers need both *desire* to have something we offer and *trust* in us to deliver, before they'll buy it.

For me, it's no different when we are selling to our people a new approach to analysing and improving our organisation.

We need to build their desire to a point where it becomes compelling.

We need to build trust to a point where there is no doubting the expected results.

How does our statement of purpose create a desire to make our organisation better? How can we use it to inspire people to get involved?

Being part of something can be a strong driver of desire. What could we do to make it possible for anyone in our organisation to get involved in improvements?

That doesn't mean we need to get everyone's opinion and input, but it could mean giving anyone the opportunity to apply to join in. Maybe we will have a committee, or group or guild within our business that will be the custodians of The Flow of Purpose. This might be a group of staff from different teams and departments who act as champions and conduits for their colleagues. Talk to your people about your new purpose and discuss what might work for you in your business to create a desire to get involved.

Trust is best created with evidence of delivery. That probably means taking a phased or iterative approach to helping purpose flow through your organisation. Great! The diagrams we use in The Flow of Purpose do just this – they start by prioritising what we need to do. That way, we can get some early wins from our work, to prove that this purpose stuff can and does make a difference.

What will work best in our organisation for sharing the evidence and building trust? Intranet? Notice board in the canteen, monthly vlog from the boss? It's worth actively planning how we will go about building trust in the changes being made. Sometimes, this can mean being honest about what was tried and didn't work, as much as the first-time success stories.

Who believes that every change will go right first time? By contrast, who believes that if we all want to make a change happen, we'll find a way to overcome obstacles? Honesty as part of trust can build a new desire to help. That's powerful.

Building a Purposeful Culture

What is culture? What is your organisation's culture? And how does that culture support or obstruct your flow of purpose?

In Part Two, I included a brief discussion on culture, and one of my favourite descriptions of company culture is "culture is how people behave when the boss isn't there". In other words, "culture" is the common internal drivers that permeate through your business.

Turning to my dictionary, it says:

Culture n. state of manners, taste and intellectual development at a time or place.

Now, that is a very interesting definition, in the context of The Flow of Purpose. Why do I say that? For me it's that "state of intellectual development" angle. Perhaps we have identified a clear sense of purpose for our organisation, but we feel our culture needs to change to support it.

For culture to change and deliver new things, our people need to go through an intellectual exercise. They need to think through, understand, rationalise, and believe in something different. But more than that, they need to feel that there is nothing to fear – an emotional angle to change.

Being clear on the purpose, the overall why, of what we're trying to achieve as a business can help with that. If we think of culture change as an intellectual exercise (as much "minds" as "hearts") then perhaps that hints as to why you can't force culture change on people. Or if we do, people resist, certainly in the short term.

What does that mean for The Flow of Purpose?

I think it means that we need to view our shiny new purpose against our current culture.

Can people understand and rationalise the purpose we've adopted, in the context of how we currently behave? If not, or we have doubts, then we need to build culture change into the set of things we need to do to use The Flow of Purpose.

If culture needs to change, explain why (to support the new purpose), listen intently (to hear people fears and brilliant ideas) and build new habits together (to create new behaviour).

Once more, there must be a hundred or a thousand books out there on habits and behaviour to give you better help than I ever could.

All that said, by its very nature, working with purpose will begin to affect your culture anyway.

Purpose after all is the explanation for why we are doing certain things a certain way and why we care. Clear, shared purpose links the hearts and minds. Our culture turns that into how we behave.

Part Three – The Practicalities

14 The Tools

There are four diagrams within The Flow of Purpose tool-set.

Broadly speaking each diagram explores and analyses it's own level of detail, plus it helps us prioritise the next level of diagram down.

This helps us to start working without having to analyse and plan everything out – whilst still being confident that we are making sensible judgements on what to do first.

That means starting with the first diagram (The Six Building Blocks of Business). We'll draw some conclusions from the work, and maybe take some questions offline for further exploration.

We'll also put the six blocks in priority order.

This allows us to go through the second, third and fourth diagrams for our top priority area.

When we have gone through all of the tools for the first priority Building Block, we can go back through the process, this time for our second priority area/block.

We repeat the process until we've used all the levels of the tools for each of the Building Blocks. To complete all the tools at all levels in all areas could

Part Three – The Practicalities

take considerable time – weeks, months or even years if there is a lot to cover in each area.

Of course, because you are working in priority order at all times, you can make a call on whether you think you've hit the law of diminishing returns. You can always re-prioritise remaining work in the more detailed diagrams.

Here is a reminder of how the tools fit together:

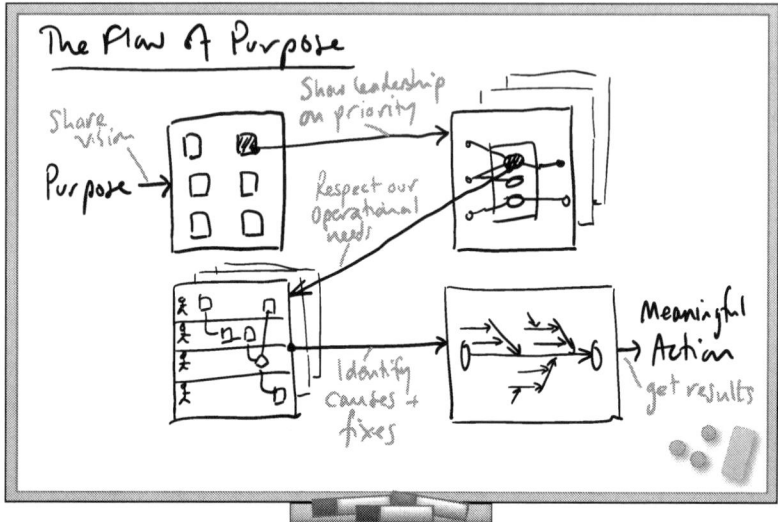

Figure 14 A reminder of how and why the diagrams work together

Part Three – The Practicalities

And pictorially, here's how the prioritised iterations work:

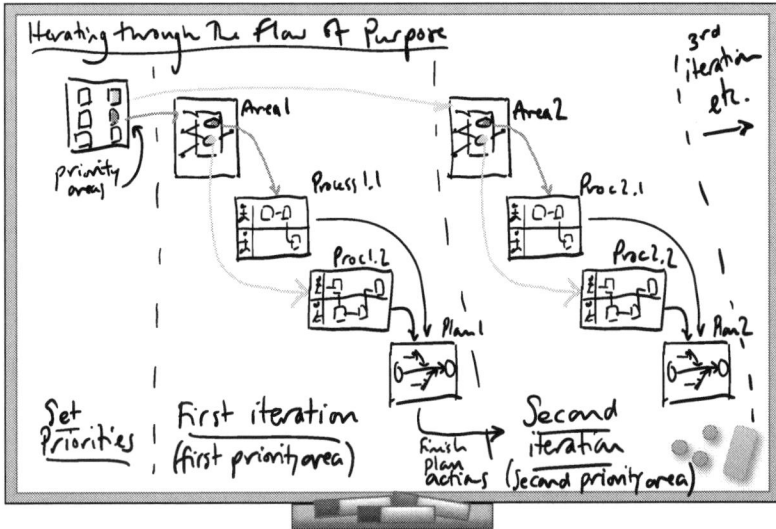

Figure 15 It's likely you'll need more than one iteration/project

Don't worry about the details of this diagram – we'll cover the them in the next section. The important thing is that it shows we can get early benefits, whilst covering all areas in the fullness of time.

Part Three – The Practicalities

Introduction

The Philosophies

The Preparation

The Practicalities

Share Priorities

Find Stakeholders

Explore Processes

Purposeful Planning

Part Three – The Practicalities

15 Share Priorities

What Is It?

We identify and share major priorities using The Six Building Blocks of Business. This is a technique used to gather people together to discuss and prioritise the main areas of the organisation.

Why Use it? Purpose & Outcomes

We use the Six Building Blocks with people across different roles and levels of responsibility, to get a broader view of changes and improvements.

We use it to challenge and explore thinking about "where our work fits with others'". This helps with discussions on priorities.

It also helps us to expose where people in different roles disagree about the importance of activities, and the amount of effort the organisation devotes to them.

How It Helps The Flow of Purpose

The Six Building Blocks of Business help The Flow of Purpose by:

- Building a single view of what and how our business works

- Creating a shared understanding of what we need from one another's areas
- Getting some of the big problems out in the open early – the "elephants in the room"
- Showing that we can't necessarily improve all areas at once, but that we work to priorities.

The Six Building Blocks (spoiler alert: or however many you actually end up with) help our team start from the same view of what we do as a business and why. It is our first opportunity to identify what areas might need attention first, in order to make the biggest positive impact to our operations and people.

By exploring and setting joint priorities, it helps the people involved in championing change to explain The Flow of Purpose links what we need to do with the big picture.

This is also an opportunity to get some early warning of the problems and challenges we might face further down the line. By observing the discussions between participants, we can begin to get a sense of how business functions see and regard one another.

If we come up against problems at this stage, we need to solve them now, before moving into the more detailed stages.

Many people start process improvement work by first delving in to the processes themselves. I've learned over the years that there can be a lot of groundwork involved beforehand. It was these lessons about getting people "on-side" before looking at process changes that planted the seeds of The Flow of Purpose in my mind.

Who Gets Involved?

The most likely people to involve in the Six Building Blocks of Business are:

- The person owning and driving the changes or improvements to the business
- The business leaders who own each of the building blocks – usually your CxOs, directors or "heads-of"
- Possibly; experienced or key staff – your "key influencers" – in the areas

- If you have a small team, you can conceivably involve them all in the Six Building Blocks exercise, with a bit more facilitation effort to make sure everyone has an appropriate say.

There are two angles to consider with the Six Building Blocks exercise. First, the people we are looking for here are those who can make the decisions on priority and effort. Second, those who can stop or derail progress through their decisions or influence.

We want to find not just the enthusiasm for change in our group, but also the potential obstacles and blockers. Leaders and experienced people can (often rightly) fear change to ways of working. Part of The Flow of Purpose is to acknowledge that concerns and fears have valid roots, and address them if needed.

A sense of purpose helps us see fears and concerns as signs of risks that we need to manage, in order to achieve our bigger objective. Put another way, we need to work out how our joint purpose compels us to work together to overcome the inevitable hurdles.

Many, many times when I have facilitated sessions like these, the participants make a point of speaking to me afterwards. A common theme I see is people telling me "It was really valuable just to spend time together as a group. We so seldom get the chance to get quality collaboration time together. I feel like we have a much clearer view of things now."

I do understand that people (and businesses) see a room full of senior people as a very expensive thing to do, and therefore costly and risky. It's not unreasonable for us to be challenged with this point if we are pulling this session together. If we are asked to explain and justify, we should aim to put across a positive case built on the likely benefits.

Another angle to try is to ask what the alternative is, and how effective will that be at solving problems? For example, instead of gathering people together for an intensive day focused on understanding how we affect one another, we could just meander on with senior people invisibly frittering away time adding to an uncontrolled, ever-growing email trail of justifications and point scoring about why they deserve priority. That sounds like an excellent approach...

Using the tool

When it's time for you to facilitate the session, gather the key people around you in a suitable meeting room. Setting the room up for round-table seating works best in my experience, but it's not vital. I would suggest leaving room for people to move around, as this lets you "pass the pen" to other people to draw and annotate. It also means that you can get people up and mingling if they are voting on things you've drawn up. This increases energy and encourages the debate and sharing of ideas.

Choose a big whiteboard, or project a whiteboard app from your computer. I'd also suggest having a second, smaller whiteboard, flipchart or screen to hand to capture side-notes.

At the top of the board, write up your organisation's statement of purpose, to remind people to focus on the big why.

Below your purpose, note down two more things: "Our outcome today..." and "because...". Talk this through with the group to make sure you use words that people buy in to. What we are looking for are variants of:

- "Our outcome today is an agreed view of our major business areas and what order we want to improve them in" and
- "because we want to start improving things quickly, by drilling down into one area at a time, in a structured and planned way."

(Note: I've not drawn "outcome" and "because" below, to save space).

Draw up a big containing box, with six smaller boxes – the basic set of key functions that I believe a business must have:

- Market
- Sell
- Do Work
- Get Paid
- Run Business
- Innovate.

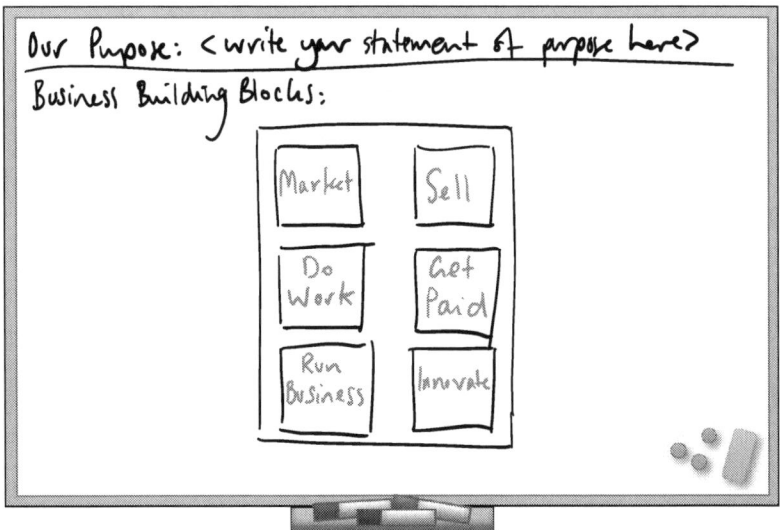

Figure 16 The Six Building Blocks of Business

Now what we need to do is discuss a little bit more about what each of these boxes means, and then ask people to think of their area's main activities, and list them against each box. We're also looking to see if we need to add any additional boxes, for example, if you have an ultra-specialised business, or want to call out a specific area, project, etc. for particular attention.

Here are my slightly more detailed introductions to what these boxes mean. At this stage, I usually start with my standard six boxes, explain them briefly, and ask people to write down what boxes they think our business would divide down into, and why. When I'm facilitating, I'm happy if we come up with a totally different set of boxes, as long as we discuss and agree them all.

Market

Market is about getting the right people to understand our message, our brand, our proposition.

This box is about things like:

- knowing who our buyers are
- what we do for them to add value (our proposition)
- how we differentiate
- how we get our message to them (content and channels)

Part Three – The Practicalities

- how we test and measure our campaigns and engagement
- how we refine our messages and propositions.

I'm sure you can think of other things. Great! Get people to shout them out and write them up. We want to help people all round the table understand what's involved here. We want people to start seeing how what one area does can affect other areas. We want to show how other people are supported or hindered.

What if you are a not-for-profit, or public sector organisation?

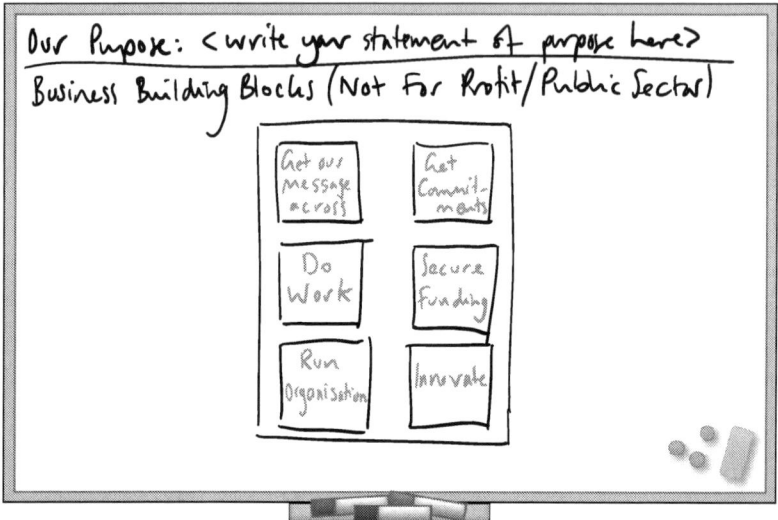

Figure 17 The Building Blocks for a Public/Not-For-Profit Organisation

Usually, not-for-profit organisations still have to get a message across to someone. It might be a very broadly applicable message, to whole sections of the country or community – advising people how and why to do something better, for example. Or, it might be a message which needs to influence a small group of stakeholders that control our funding, if your work is a bit more "under the radar". The key point of interest in this box is that it's about getting people to receive our message; and you being confident that it has been received. What could we use to measure that?

Sell

Selling is about helping people who have understood our marketing messages to commit to buying from us (or making some other form of commitment). It is about making the promises we covered when we discussed desire and trust.

I'd normally seed this box's discussion with activities like:

- Sales calls and meetings
- Listening and establishing customer needs and desires
- Product or service demonstrations and proofs of concept
- Creating vision with customers of what our offerings could do for them
- Creating proposals, responding to tender requests and so on
- Handling objections and answering questions – working out how trust will be gained
- Negotiating and agreeing commercials – making the actual promises.

Once again, we want your sales-related people shouting things out for you to write, and the other people in the room asking questions and making suggestions.

If you are facilitating this Six Building Blocks session, you can be as blunt as asking people to ask questions of each other, or you could ask for noteworthy sales experiences they've had recently. "Noteworthy" could be good or bad of course... How does the sales process compare to the shared examples?

Of course, this idea of asking questions and sharing experience can be used for all six of the boxes. At this stage, what we are trying to do is get as much information as we can on the board about the things we do. These notes will be the raw material for the discussions on priorities and effort needed.

Here's what your board might look like when you capture such Q&A and experience information (zoomed in for artistic and dramatic effect...):

Part Three – The Practicalities

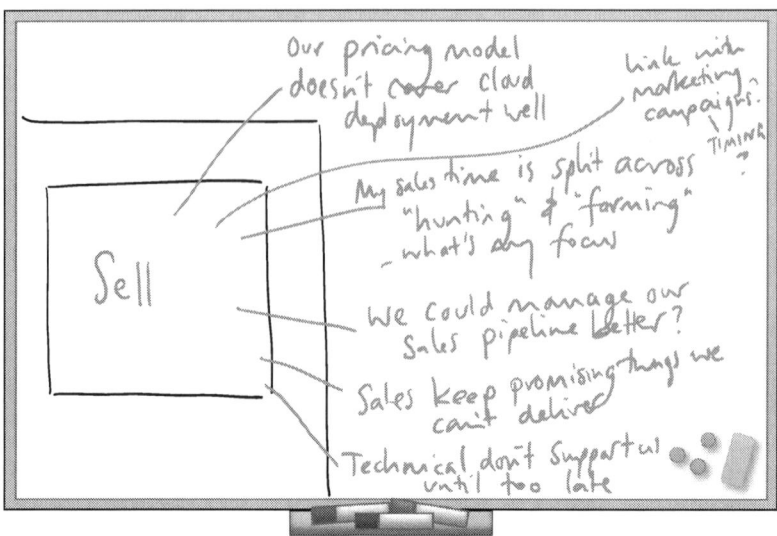

Figure 18 Dramatic close-up of example notes, ideas & feedback

Selling as a box might feel like it has no place if your organisation is a not-for-profit, charity or public sector body. It might be appropriate to remove it as a building block, but have a think before you remove it completely. You might prefer to rename it as something like "Convince" or "Get Commitment". You may be convincing people to donate to your cause. You may be convincing funders of the merit of your proposal. It can be worth debating this point with your group, to underline that most organisations need some aspect of selling skills in-house (or outsourced) to be sustainable.

Do Work

Doing work is the provision of the product or service that delivers the value the customer committed to pay for. It is keeping the promise we made in the sales process, if you prefer.

When I'm presenting this Building Block I normally explain that I see both initial work and ongoing support activities as "Do Work" – but as a group, we could decide that there is a case to subdivide Do Work as needed. My advice here, is to be led by your customer's experience. If they feel like they are buying two different things – implementation then support, then by all means split this down – as long as you debate and agree the split.

The topics you note against Do Work will depend upon what your offerings are, but here are some ideas to stimulate your group discussions:

- Work, production or resource planning and scheduling
- Job and task management
- Staff management and mentoring
- Stock management
- Product assembly, service delivery or project activities
- Client engagement around our work – e.g. clarifying needs, communicating progress, getting feedback, etc.
- Adjustments and rework to meet customer "specification"
- Travel and facilitation of client-site work
- Etc.

You may want to remind people that the reason we are digging into our building blocks as a group is to make sure we all understand what one another does. Often, by this point, we are having some healthy debate about the exact relationships between marketing messages, sales promises and operational delivery...

Ask "what do we do then?" and "why?" a lot. (And remember, as the debate intensifies, facilitation is a fun and valuable activity!)

You may find it useful to have a second whiteboard, or flipchart to note down actions for people to "take offline" – things we identify as needing to be done, but not really core to what we are discussing right now. This helps you park needlessly contentious points, if they are not helping us in our overall goal to get broad understanding and priorities. You may need to make a facilitator's judgement call on whether something needs to be explored now, or if we are getting into too much detail.

This section can get quite emotional – either heated or excited. Use your ace facilitation skills to keep the energy positive. We're pulling out these problems to solve them. We're sharing these ideas to focus on the most feasible and rewarding. We're looking to spot our problems and fix them before the customer sees them. Sharing honest, constructive opinions can be difficult but is worthwhile. *(Note: I'm writing this in the UK, where we sometimes have a habit of not wanting to appear too critical, if you don't mind me putting it that way, although of course, it could be me that's wrong, etc., etc.).*

Get Paid

I hummed and hawed about splitting "Get Paid" out as a separate building block. You could argue that it fits under Run Business, or possibly even Do Work as a neat last step.

In the end, I put getting paid as a separate building block, for two reasons. First, bad cashflow can kill good businesses. Second, in my experience, a lot of businesses are not good, confident or disciplined at chasing payment, or have business models that make it difficult to have money in the bank early.

This building block is here as a challenge, to get our business to state and recognise how it stays sustainable with cashflow, and to ask "could we do it better"?

Here are some of the areas I typically ask about and explore with cashflow:

- At what point (in our processes/engagements) do we get money in the bank for our offerings?
- How predictable is our cashflow (even if we are paid in arrears)?
- Is cashflow reliable, or are we always wondering who we need to chase next?
- Could we get paid earlier; some or all of the bill?
- What would stop us doing that? (e.g. never tried it, customers reject it [evidence?], low trust in industry [in us?], etc.)
- What precedents are there in our or other industries for incentives or new ways of buying that would get us cash earlier, or more predictably?
- Can we offer our product on some sort of subscription basis to get paid every month?
- Can we split offerings up into stages or subscription-plus-purchase models?
- Why did we pick this business model? What has changed in the world/our industry since we picked this model?
- Is there any way that getting cash in the bank is connected to purpose, for our customers?

Often, this area feels like it will be a really quick one to cover. However, it can generate some interesting ideas to take offline. It's common to need to investigate things a bit more for this block. Here's a thought to put to your group: some businesses are very focused on cashflow, getting paid up front and paying for their growth organically – how close do we think we could get our business, or even one of our offerings, to being paid up-front?

Run Business

When we run a business, we have a range of administrative and compliance activities. They tend to change as you grow and depending on the industry you are in.

These are often activities you can't get away without doing – but that doesn't mean you have to do them yourselves. You could outsource some of these, to get a better, cheaper and less risky service than doing things internally. The debate around this box can help draw out ideas for streamlining and outsourcing. It can also be useful to identify risks that you now have due to growth.

Here are some topics to get you started with your group brainstorming and debate. Augment as you see fit:

- Accounting – annual accounts, profit-and-loss, balance sheet, management accounts – go through the who, why, what, where, when and how of making and using them.
- Taxes and legals – how do you plan for, manage and pay taxes, how do you approach compliance with regulation around your product or service offering?
- Health and safety – setting, monitoring and reporting – why, where, who and how, especially.
- What are your people-related activities, like general HR, recruitment, disciplinaries, holidays, sickness, etc.
- How do you do time and performance tracking? Does it work, do you do anything with the data, do you find people are more motivated and perform better? What would you change if you needed to do better?
- Skills and training – how do you make sure your people know enough to work at the level you need them to? How much of this do you invest in compared to your competitors?
- Security and data protection – who owns these, is there an understanding of the risks and penalties involved in these with recent developments around the world – for example the massive fines possible under the EU's General Data Protection Regulations?

- Information and Communication Technologies – is your IT an enabler for every other building block, or has it been relegated to a cost-driven compliance function?

The Building Blocks exercise is an opportunity for your group members to see what is supported and enabled by (sometimes much maligned) central functions. It can help to see the value that they add and so help to make a case for investing time and thought in them.

On the flip-side, in a centrally-driven, command-and-control type organisation, going through the building blocks together can help strong central functions people see how their influence and control can restrict what other parts of the business can do to respond to customer, market and competitor developments.

I'd suggest that you resist any temptation to skip over debate about "Run Business", by dismissing it as "just admin"... Use pointed questions to constructively challenge people who resist!

Innovate

I originally called this Building Block "Develop Product/Service", but that was too long. Clear though... In fact, if you think it sits better with your organisation, then write the box up as "Develop Product". I know that "innovation" can sometimes be seen as a bit of a nebulous word (though it shouldn't be, I believe!).

The point we need to cover here is that to stay relevant, what we offer needs to change and get updated. Even if we have a market-leading offering right now, customer needs change, markets change, and new competitors appear.

To me, that means devoting time, effort and money to consciously adapt and improve what we offer to customers.

With this building block, we want to explore how purposeful our innovation is. Are we driven by our organisation's purpose, our customers' purpose? If we feel we don't have organisational purpose, will looking at how and why we innovate help us find our purpose?

Here are some questions to start your group brainstorming:

- Who is responsible for developing/innovating?

Part Three – The Practicalities

- What triggers us to develop something new? Is it scheduled? Based on a new idea? Market-driven? Customer-requests?
- Where does our organisational purpose (or vision/mission) fit into our innovation or product development process? Who judges the fit to purpose/vision?
- How do we decide what to develop and what to leave – i.e. what is the "why" we use to judge if development is worth it?
- Who's going to buy our new offering? How do we go about finding this out?
- What modelling do we do around the impact of an innovation or development?
- How much time do we devote to innovation? Why is it this amount? Do we feel it's enough? Too much? Why?
- How much effort goes into protecting our innovation (intellectual property)?
- Who do we involve in developing new offerings? Why? How does that work?
- What approach do we use to maximise the chances of product developments being successful? (e.g. do we have cross-functional teams? Work in Agile ways? Do business cases? Incentivise key staff? Engage third party experts? Create Minimum Viable Products (MVPs) and market test, etc.
- Are we constrained by compliance "boundaries"? Could we reduce their impact, or remove them, even if temporarily? Would that unlock any value (e.g. by creating new ideas)?
- How well has innovation and new development worked so far? How have we fared when taking the new things "out of the lab and onto the street"?
- Have we been able to market, sell, deliver and support the innovations we created? How did we need to adapt our ways of working to do this?

If you read Part Two before coming to this section on the tools, you may recall my suggestion that innovation is all about giving customers new things to buy from us, or new reasons to stay with us. So what we need to explore together is how we ensure we meet that need. How do we collaborate so that we are responding to changes in our customers' needs, with things that they feel compelled to buy, in a way that means we make more profit (or show more value)?

Any More Building Blocks Needed?

As I said in the intro to this section, I'm fairly confident that most activities, for most businesses, will fit into one of the six "standard" Building Blocks. It's how you do them, and why (purpose...) that makes you different.

But there are cases where people in the group demand that you draw up more blocks. That's absolutely OK. By all means make it a debate if you want to challenge someone on that assertion. It's much more important to have discussion and information written up than to have an arbitrary number of boxes on a whiteboard.

When someone asks for a new box, essentially they are saying "I want some special treatment or recognition", and we're asking "do you really need that?"

They might do.

I've worked with some quite specialist businesses, who were trying to get to grips with challenges in the particular area of the business that made them specialists.

Since we all had a strong suspicion that many of the problems (and opportunities) were in that one area, certainly in the short term, we gave it a Building Block all of its own.

You might do a similar thing if you have a massive, high-impact project coming up. Something like implementing a new CRM system, a new ERP (Enterprise Resource Planning) system, or a merger or acquisition. Give it its own building block.

Part Three – The Practicalities

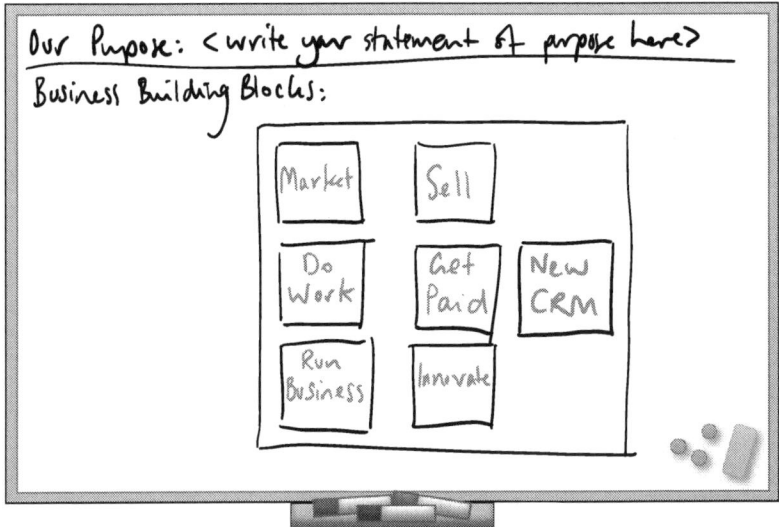

Figure 19 Adding your own Building Block for major items. We're going to need a bigger box...

Why would you do this?

Well, the whole reason we're going through the Building Blocks is to understand how we work together and affect one another's areas, so we can explore and set shared priorities.

For example, rather than try to argue which of the standard blocks happens to have the highest number of priority CRM items spread through it, let's extract those CRM priorities and gather them together.

This does a few things:

- It shows visually that most things we do (the other boxes) are OK, but we need to get this one thing (CRM) done in its own right.
- If it's a project type box, we can set a deadline, timeline or criteria for when we remove the extra block – priorities change over time after all. Especially when we've addressed the things that made an area our first priority.
- Having a separate CRM block in our diagram implies that someone needs to own it, and that all the standard blocks need to contribute to the success of the extra block (and vice versa) – it doesn't exist in isolation.

Part Three – The Practicalities

If you feel you need another block, go ahead and add it to the diagram, and repeat the brainstorming exercise you've done for the standard boxes. Make sure you note the purpose of splitting out the box beside it – the "why" that ultimately supports your organisation's purpose.

Perhaps some of the existing notes and items you've covered and drawn up will migrate to this new box. You may even identify what sorts of conversations should be happening between the new building block owner, and the ones you've already identified. Setting these regular meetings, calls or reports up might be a "take offline" action you note on your second whiteboard.

As you go or at the end, try to capture the decisions and essence of discussions around the creation of the new building block. Share these notes with the group so we remember why and how we created the new block.

Discuss, Vote on Priorities and Summarise

Let's recap. At this stage, you should be looking at a whiteboard with six or more big boxes on it. Each box should have against it a load of notes, thoughts, questions and ideas. There may also be a name against each box for who owns the area, even if just for the purposes of this exercise.

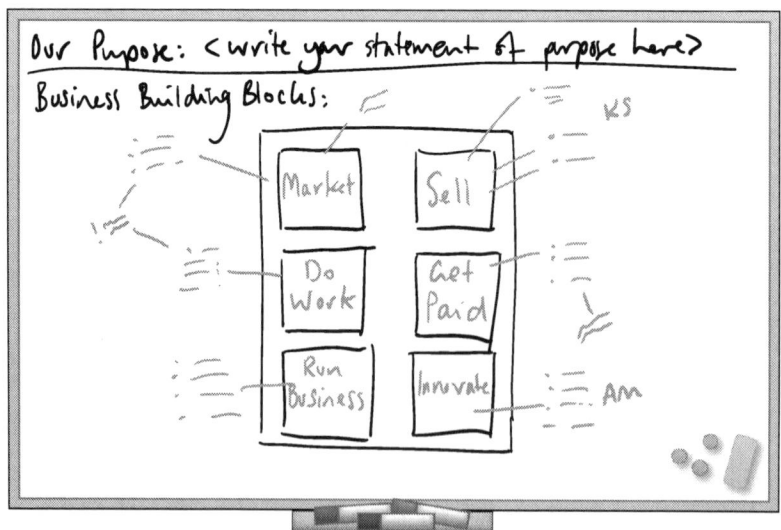

Figure 20 Building Blocks with notes - you'll probably have more detail

Part Three – The Practicalities

There will probably have been a good amount of discussion, debate, and questioning. A few people might have had a huff or a hissy fit.

You're probably also quite tired...

I sometimes take a short break at this point, to let everything cogitate through people's minds. This is a judgement call though. If you fear that people will get dragged out of the session into emails or calls or "urgent stuff," then you may want to press on instead, and maintain the momentum. You know your organisation better than me. You can even ask people if they want to keep going rather than take a break. Without overthinking it, in itself, the way that people answer you could tell you about their commitment to driving purpose through the business.

Anyway, the next step is to try to pull together all these great ideas and discussions into an agreed priority list.

Here's my go-to approach for doing this – adapt it as you see fit to work for your audience. I do it this way so that everyone gets a say, people have time to think, and we get a chance to share what we've been thinking even if we haven't voiced it yet. Here's how it works:

- Everyone gets a set number of "votes" – sometimes these are marks I draw up on the board, or you can give people sticky dots (or whiteboard magnets, etc.) to vote with. 3-5 votes is usually enough.
- We go round the table to take first votes. Each person picks a Building Block to get their vote for it being a priority.
- They also have to say a sentence or so that explains their thinking for it being a priority (a chance to share thinking, especially for introverts in the group – stereotyping enormously here).
- I try to avoid too much discussion at this stage, but sometimes have a "hand up to ask a question" rule, so that we can manage any genuine questions with immediate answers, or take offline – this part is about people's opinions rather than debate and justification.
- We move on to the next person for them to cast their vote and explain their thinking.
- We go round the table until everyone has cast their first vote.
- We repeat this exercise, one vote at a time, until everyone has used all their votes. It is OK for someone to vote for the same thing more than once to show they really, really think it's a priority.
- It's also OK for some blocks to have no votes.

When all votes have been cast, count up the total votes for each block, and note the number against the box.

Now list the block names in descending score order – your highest scoring block is first and is your top priority area.

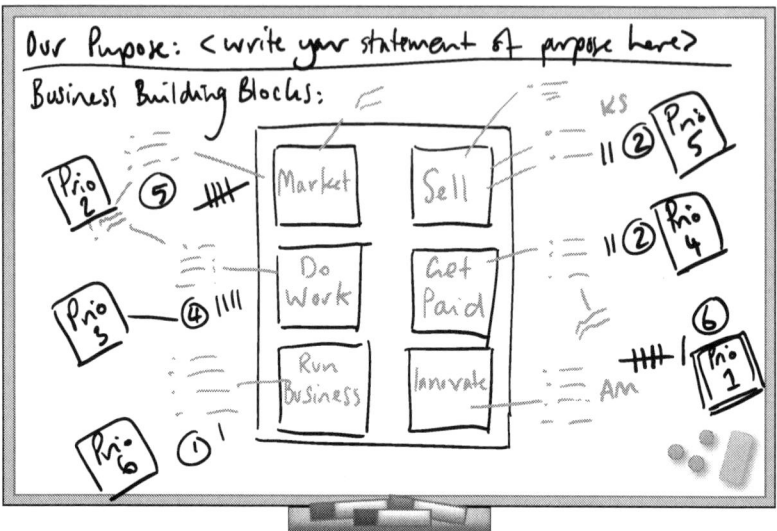

You might want to take a minute or two to discuss any surprises or note any lingering concerns (as offline actions with owners and dates…)

You are ready for the next step – what to do with the outputs.

Variations

Before skipping on to that next step, just a few words on some variations on the voting and prioritisation.

Red & Green Votes: Nothing to do with socialist or environmental politics! You can give people a number of "red and green votes" instead of just single votes. Why might you do this? A "green vote" is given where a person believes a building block is good enough for now, and doesn't need any fixing. A "red vote" is like the ones I described in the guide above – a vote for something that is a concern and needs fixed. This two-colour approach can help with getting people positive about parts of the business, if the atmosphere has been a bit down-beat or frustrated. It can also expose areas where understanding might be lacking – if an area has a mix of green and red votes,

Part Three – The Practicalities

then the implication is that we are not viewing that area consistently. This warrants some offline discussion... For your vote totals, green votes have a score of -1 and red votes +1; highest total score is the highest priority in this case too (i.e. highest score needs the most fixing).

Mingle and Stick: The Mingle and Stick is not a town-centre theme pub. Instead I alluded to this approach in my guide above when I mentioned sticky dots or whiteboard magnets. You'll have less control with this method, but more energy in the room. In this model, you explain the rules, and let people get up and physically place their votes. Restrict the supply of dots/magnets unless you fully trust people... The rules are very similar – you can put one or more votes against the things that you feel are the highest priority (or lowest if you are using red/green sticky dots to do red/green voting too). I encourage people to discuss with the people around them why they are voting the way they are, so we keep the spirit of communication going. You might even finish up this style of voting by sitting down again and going round the table for people to summarise in a sentence or two their thoughts around the voting.

What To Do With The Outputs

The primary reason for doing the Building Blocks of Business is to prioritise which areas of your business to investigate and improve first, given your purpose.

There are other useful things that can come out of the exercise too.

You can build on the group discussions, to identify ways we help and hinder one another across area boundaries. If we recognise that we have a problem, we can start to think about how to solve it. That's a lot of what the follow-on tools are designed to do, but if a quick win suggests itself at this stage, it might be worth giving it a try, as long as it is in line with your purpose.

In a similar way, you can look for interdependencies between areas that might not have been clear before. Were there any lightbulb moments during the discussions about why things go wrong, take longer than they feel they should or need rescuing somewhere down the line? Can you spot what linkages there are that create the issues? We'll look for these in detail in the Process Flows, but this is an opportunity to capture any initial ideas.

I'd also suggest that you schedule a regular review of your Building Blocks. Maybe every 6-12 months your leadership group can get together around the whiteboard, and review where things currently stand with your areas and priorities. How has the work you've been doing affected the relative priorities? Is there a need to discuss, debate and vote again?

A fascinating (for me) thing to try with the Building Blocks is to work out what percentage of our organisation's effort goes into each box. We may need to analyse timesheet data or similar to get these figures. Do the numbers provide any surprises? Do we think the percentages might need to change to accommodate forthcoming work or changes? I find this an interesting exercise to do, because I work with such a broad array of businesses. As you might imagine, the percentage splits across boxes vary with organisational size, lifecycle stage (pre-startup, startup, growth, mature, etc.), industry and so on. There's probably a whole other book in that, to be honest.

What next?

We use the priority list we've created to set the order in which we explore the business areas (the boxes in our diagram). Ideally, we go through all The Flow of Purpose tools for the first priority area, making a good amount of progress, before reviewing the priorities and starting on the other areas.

That means the main thing to do next is to plan and work through using the remaining Flow of Purpose tools for your highest priority area first. The next chapters explain how to use the other Flow of Purpose tools.

A note: Once you've run through the following Flow of Purpose stages, you'll have a Purpose Driven Plan for actions related to your highest priority area. You can get started on that, and when you've finished, or made enough progress, you can come back to this point, and repeat the overall process for your second and subsequent priority areas, until you've gone through all six areas (building block boxes).

For now, you may want to prepare for the next tool by organising the next step's workshop or session for the top priority Building Block. Invite the key people who are involved in and affected by the Building Block. This may be the same people as have been in the initial session, a subset of them, or a subset of them plus some other key people that weren't in the original session. We'll go into that in a bit more detail in the next chapter.

Remember that it can also be worthwhile to share a summary of the session and some detail on the outcomes across your entire team. We are after all starting to talk about a shared purpose and how it fits our ways of working. If people feel at least some sense of involvement from the start, then changes will be less of a surprise. People may even end up looking forward to getting involved in giving them a try.

With the output from the Building Blocks of Business, and the workshop you have set up, we are now ready to move to the next Flow of Purpose Tool – People & Processes – so we can identify our stakeholders.

Part Three – The Practicalities

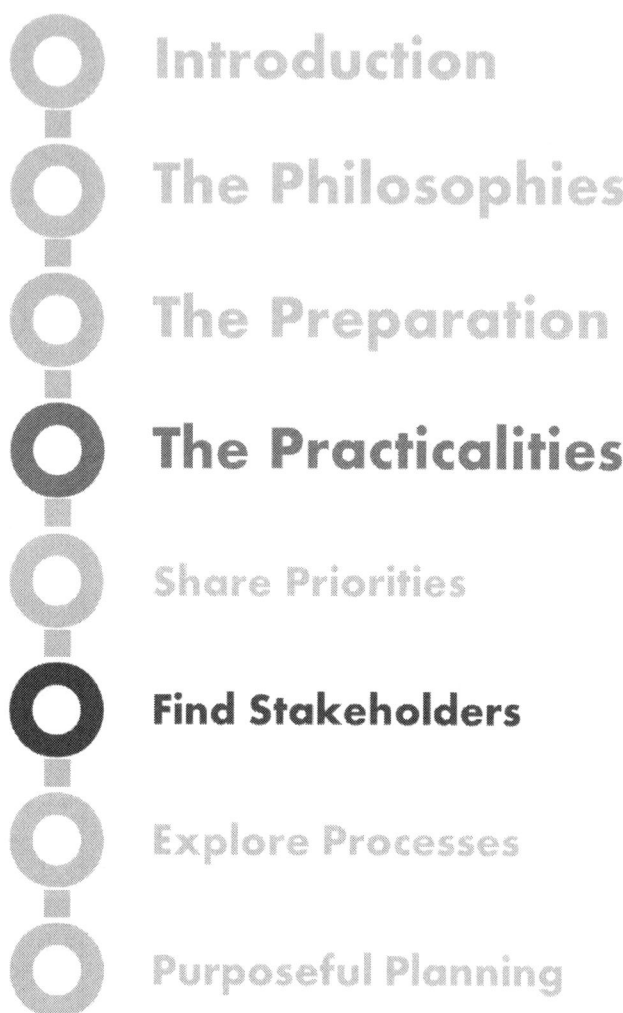

Introduction

The Philosophies

The Preparation

The Practicalities

Share Priorities

Find Stakeholders

Explore Processes

Purposeful Planning

Part Three – The Practicalities

16 Find Stakeholders

What Is It?

We identify, discuss and understand the needs of our stakeholders using People & Processes.

People & Processes is the second level of analysis tool, after the Building Blocks of Business. People & Processes takes a single Building Block, and breaks it down into major processes, and connects them with the roles, partners and systems that use them.

Why Use it? Purpose & Outcomes

We use People & Processes to prioritise processes for further exploration, much like we used the Building Blocks to prioritise areas of the business.

People & Processes also helps us to work out who our stakeholders are. Stakeholders are those roles (people) and external parties (suppliers, service providers, regulatory bodies and so on) that give or get something from us as we operate.

Lastly, we can start to get a view for what interfaces and exchanges of information we have between the roles, partners and systems involved in this process area. In this context, an interface could be a conversation, a phone call, letter, email or electronic computer interface.

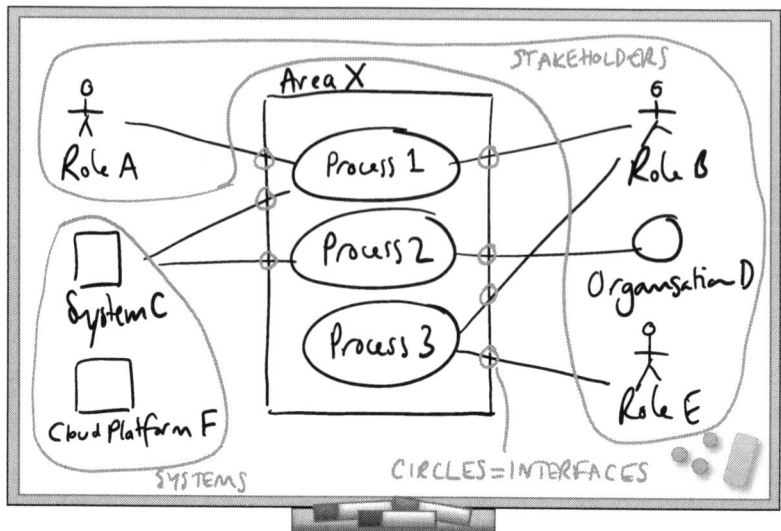

Figure 21 Processes, Stakeholders, Systems and Interfaces for this area

How It Helps The Flow of Purpose

Breaking down our business areas (Building Blocks) into processes helps us to ask for each "why do we do this – how does it contribute to our purpose?" In turn, this helps us change our processes over time, so that they are more clearly linked with our overall purpose. We may decide to change our processes, start doing new things, or stop (or outsource) processes that are not core to our purpose.

Using People & Processes also allows us to explore what the relationships are between our people and stakeholders, and our purpose. Do the people in the roles understand that they have a part to play in delivering our purpose?

If we include the systems we use in People & Processes, this helps us establish if they are truly fit for purpose. Does their functionality and performance help us or hinder us in delivering our purpose?

Are we passing and using the right information? Why are we gathering some data but not others? How does the information fit our purposes – do we have

Part Three – The Practicalities

gaps or unnecessary excess? We can get valuable clues to these questions by going through People & Processes.

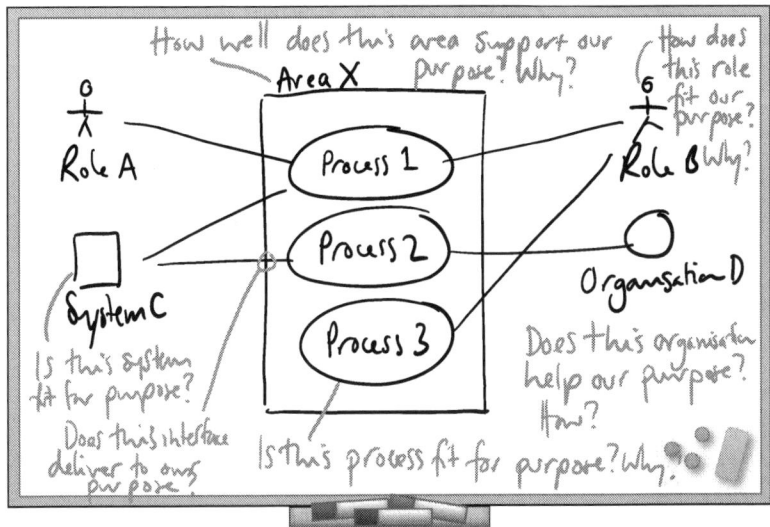

Figure 22 Example considerations for People & Process. And Systems & Interfaces...

Who Gets Involved?

To get the most out of People & Processes, you'll need a few different types of people.

We'll need the person or people who have accountability for the overall business area. They matter because they have the authority to make decisions but may not fully know the day to day detail. This person "owns the box" in the diagram.

Senior operational staff – managers or experienced workers – will help to bring real-world experience to the group discussions. These people need to be familiar with how we actually work, not just what the process manual says. If we have a formal Subject Matter Expert role in our organisation, they're quite likely to be involved with the People & Processes exercise for their area. Team Leaders are another good source of real-world experience. These are people who "own or drive the blobs" in our diagram.

If possible, it can be useful to have specific experts on hand, on the phone or ready to be dragged in to the workshop for 10 minutes. Doing so can save a lot of to-and-fro and conjecture on specific points that we raise with one another. It also helps people feel involved and listened to. What I tend to do here is hijack a few minutes in a team meeting, maybe a week before. I explain what the session is going to be about, and that we might need to get some detailed information. If that's the case, I'll grab one of the team for a few minutes. It's nothing to be worried about, and equally, if we don't call anyone in, that's still OK.

Using the tool

People & Processes looks absurdly simple in action. That doesn't mean it's not useful. And of course, the discussion the tool provokes is as useful as the diagram we end up drawing.

Here's how we use it.

Gather your group together, with a big whiteboard or electronic equivalent. I also recommend having a separate whiteboard, screen or flipchart for noting items to action "offline".

Write your organisation's statement of purpose at the top of the board to keep people focused on why we do what we do, the way we do it.

Below your purpose, note down "Our outcome today..." and "because...". Finish the sentences with words that the group agrees with. What we are looking for are variants of:

- "Our outcome today is a prioritised view of the major things we do, who gets involved (and why), and the types of information we share" and
- "because this will help us identify who to involve in detailed process work, and major things to talk about with them."

Now we're clear on those, draw up a big box to represent the Business Building Block we're working on in this iteration. I've called it "Area X" in the diagram below, but it will be "Market", "Sell", "Do Work" or so on, depending on the names you've used.

Part Three – The Practicalities

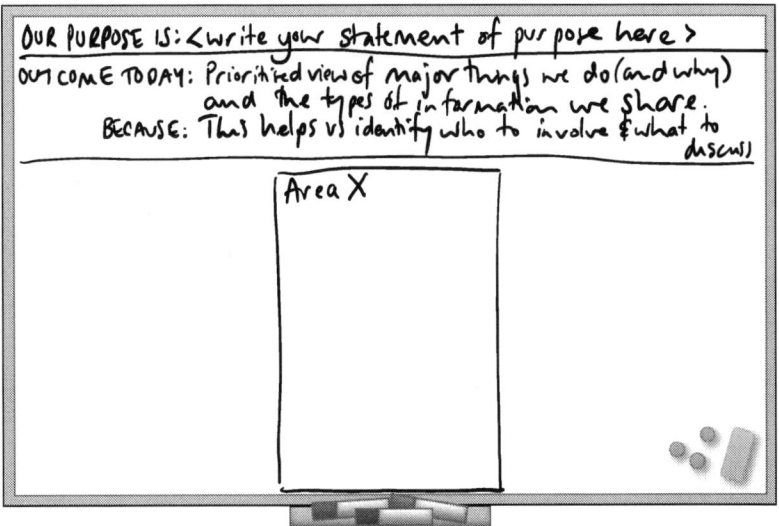

Figure 23 Start with purpose and a context (box) for the processes

This is where we go through some brainstorming and back-and-forth with the group to identify what major processes we do within the building block area, and the roles, organisations and systems that engage with the processes.

We're looking to end up with 3-7 major processes in our box. If you end up having more, consider if you can consolidate some of them; or you could split your box into two, and go through the exercise twice. The information we are interested in at this stage is who gets involved, why, and what types of information are flowing around. The next tool deals with the detail of processes.

When you identify and agree your process areas, draw them up as titled blobs within your outer box.

Part Three – The Practicalities

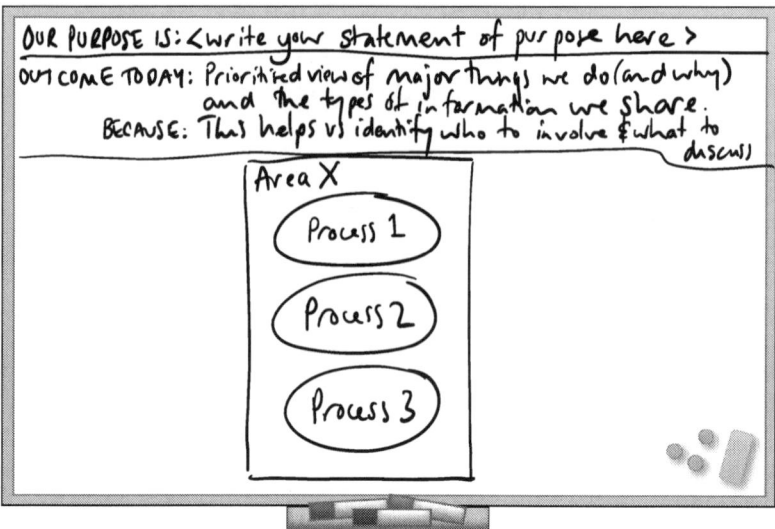

Figure 24 First break the area into 3-7 major processes

For each of the blobs, now think about who is linked to it, for what purpose.

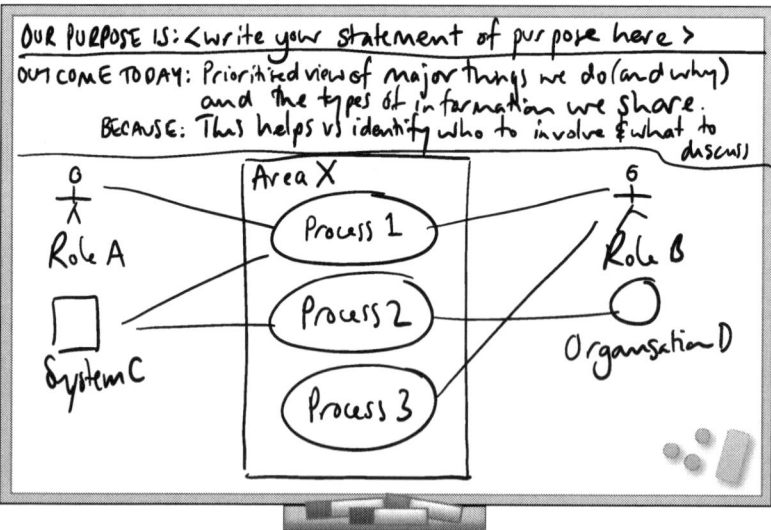

Figure 25 Add in the relationships with Stakeholders, Systems and third parties

The "who" could be a person, role, organisation, or system – we are looking for entities that need information or decisions from you, or give you information or decisions.

Incidentally, when thinking of people, try to go with roles rather than actual people. A person can have many roles, or one role can be done by one person. If you do feel that putting a single person's name on the board is the only option, then take an offline action for someone...

Why? We may have a key part of our process as an undocumented role, which is stored solely in the head of one person, and this would be a big risk to explore.

The connecting line or link is an information operation or decision relationship. This relationship could be someone supervising or managing the process, like a director. It could be someone who needs information to complete a task that they do, perhaps passing back an update to us, like a field worker might do. It could be an external organisation that checks compliance, like inland revenue, tax or health and safety authorities. It could even be a computer system like a CRM, cloud storage system, or finance system, for example.

As you identify these entities, write them up outside the box, and draw lines from them to all of the process blobs they get involved in.

If you can, try to note against each line why the link exists – just a few words. How do these whys compare to the overall purpose for our organisation, and the purpose of the process blob? Is it a compelling reason to be involved, or is it just being nosey? This can seed thinking on whether we could simplify the number of roles or systems involved in processes.

Part Three – The Practicalities

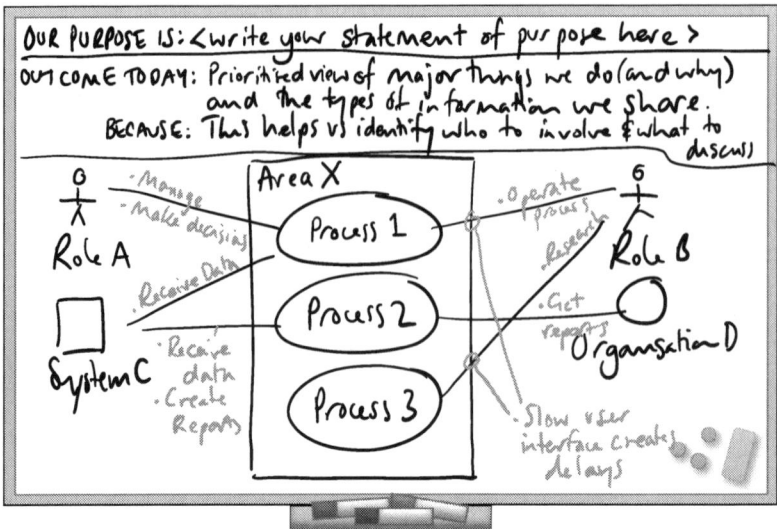

Figure 26 Noting the purpose of relationships, roles and others

Before we move on from the lines, they hint at another thing to explore – interfaces. Note against the line how the relationship uses information. Again, just a few words at most. Something like "reviewed on PC screen", "via phone call", "nightly data sync" or similar. This can start us thinking about how well that interface works for passing information quickly and reliably. Is the interface too simple? Too complex? Unreliable? Too manual? Too automated?

One final note on interfaces/relationships. I've talked about information as the thing that passes across the interface, but if you're in manufacturing or logistics, etc. then it could be materials that pass back and forth. I've spent most of my time working with information businesses, hence this bias in my approach and writing. However, many of the techniques I use actually have their underlying or historic bases in manufacturing environments.

Carry on brainstorming processes (blobs), roles/systems (titles outside box) and relationships (lines) until you run out of valuable things to say, or time. You often find that there will be adjustment of the blobs as we talk through why roles get involved, and the addition of new roles/systems as we discuss the full extent of who we work with.

At the end of this process, you could end up with quite a busy diagram, with a fair bit of information noted against it. Great! These are all opportunities to dig into things in more detail later on.

To create clarity, and help support subsequent detail work, we're back to voting again – or whatever means works for you to prioritise the blobs. We're asking people to vote on what gives them the most concern, or where they think we will benefit most from improvements.

I shared some of my thoughts on voting techniques in the Six Building Blocks of Business earlier, but here's a brief recap. Give each participant a number of votes, e.g. 3-5. Go round the group, one by one, and ask them where they put one of their votes, to show which item they think most needs attention, and why. They can vote for different or the same items in subsequent rounds. At the end, the item with the most votes is the one to explore first.

In this vote, most of the time, the votes are cast against the process blobs – the things that happen (or don't happen) in there tend to be what worries most people. I do say to people though that it is valid to put a vote against a role/system or relationship line – if you feel or know that there are particular things about it that are breaking, delaying or otherwise being all nasty and negative. Just because we're talking process, doesn't mean we should pass up the opportunity to call out things like system/interface performance, contractual issues or attitude/cultural differences. Start from your purpose and think laterally about what helps or hinders it in this Building Block/area.

Part Three – The Practicalities

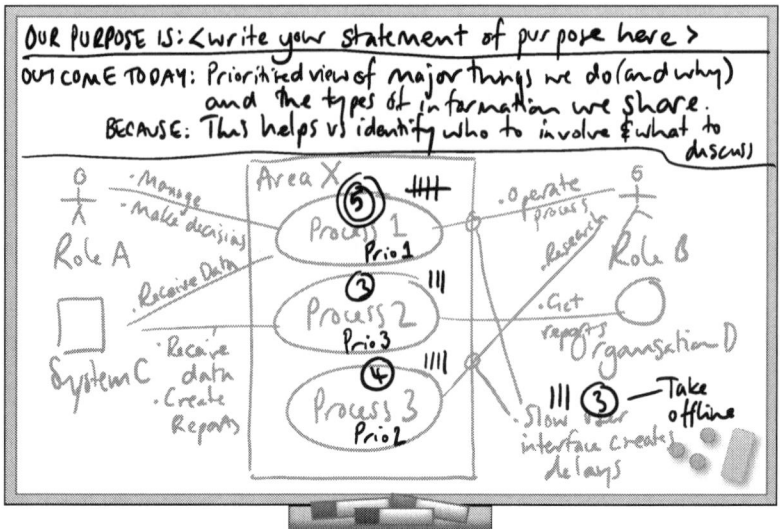

Figure 27 Work out your priorities for the next stage - or offline actions

What To Do With The Outputs

From a Flow of Purpose perspective, we use the outputs of People & Processes to do a few things. We get a sense of the priority order for exploring processes in detail (the next stage). We have created a list of people and organisations to involve, speak to or contact for each process area. We have a list of the interfaces (formal or not) that pass information, and which we need to look at to see if they speed up, slow down or muddle our processes or information.

We may also have some actions noted down which people are going to take offline.

You may want to use your interface/relationship notes (the ones against the lines) to plan separate analysis work on the detail of those interfaces. I don't explicitly cover interfaces in The Flow of Purpose, but you can use tools like SIPOC (a tool often used in TQM/Lean/Six Sigma) to get into the detail of information formats and flows. Alternatively, in the next Flow of Purpose tool (Process Flows), you can note against the links between steps details of information passed.

Part Three – The Practicalities

What next?

We'll be looking at the processes in the next stage of The Flow of Purpose, using the Process Flows tool. This is when we get down into the detail of process steps, who does them, and where the problems and opportunities lie.

Your next task in the process is to organise more group sessions. These will be in the order defined by the People & Process priority voting you've just done. They will probably involve different people in each session, driven by the stakeholders and systems you identified in your People & Processes diagram.

Let's find out what we do in these sessions...

Part Three – The Practicalities

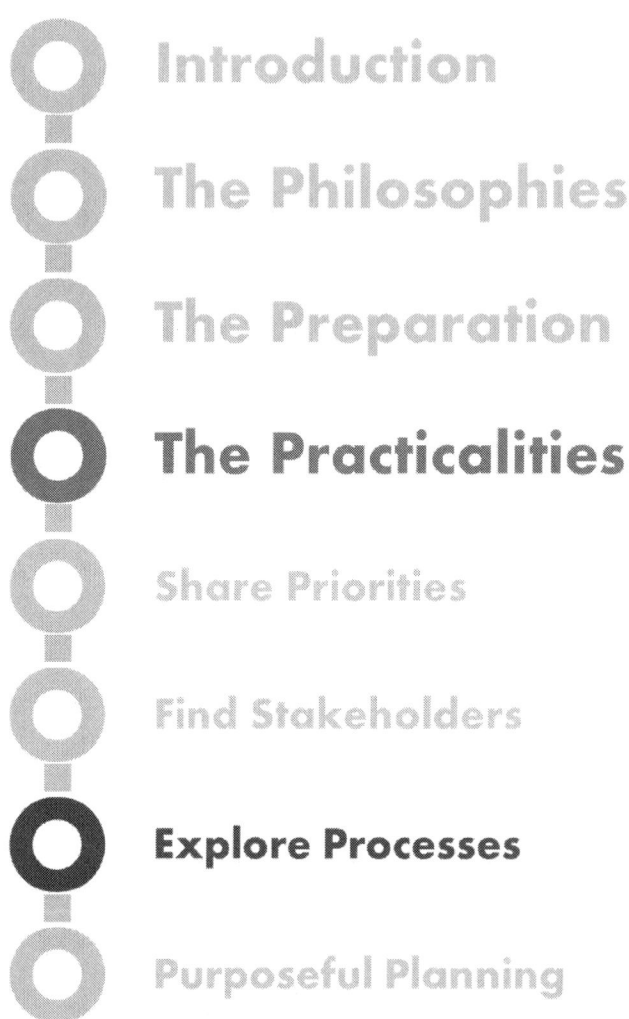

Introduction

The Philosophies

The Preparation

The Practicalities

Share Priorities

Find Stakeholders

Explore Processes

Purposeful Planning

Part Three – The Practicalities

17 Explore Processes

What Is It?

Process Flows is the tool we use to explore processes and break them down into steps, according to who does the step. We use it to look for problems, delays, bottlenecks and opportunities to improve and streamline how we work. We use "cross-functional diagrams" or "swimlane diagrams" to help us.

Why Use it? Purpose & Outcomes

This is the nitty gritty stage of analysing and improving our ways of working.

We use Process Flows to explore what the root causes might be for the bigger picture issues we see. We also use it to find specific actions we can take to improve processes by adding, changing or removing process steps.

Part Three – The Practicalities

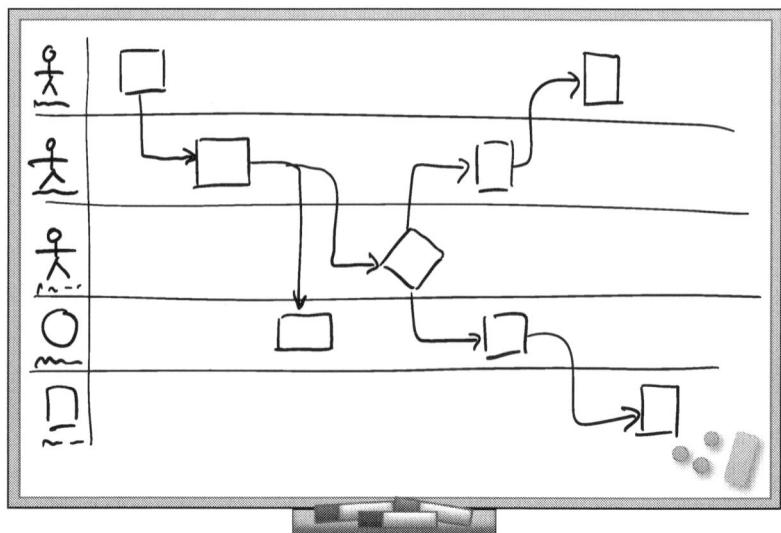

Figure 28 An overview of Process Flows - the Cross-Functional Diagram

This is often the point that a lot of people choose to start exploring processes.

Hopefully, if you've gone through the first two stages to get here, you'll see the benefits of starting with Business Building Blocks and People & Processes. These first two tools create a shared view of what we do, agreed overall priorities, and identified the people we need to talk to (and about what) at this stage.

Before we go on - if you are tempted to jump in at this stage, beware that there are risks to doing so.

- Without a common view of what the business does and why, business owners and leaders could react negatively to conclusions and ideas that you bring to them.
- Without joint prioritisation, you may find that your decision on what to look at first is open to criticism.
- Without having analysed who to involve, you risk doing a load of work only to find that some key roles weren't represented and so you have gaps in understanding and draw incorrect conclusions.

Now that I've just nagged you like a narky parent, I should of course say that you know your business best, so make the call that you feel is right. You might choose to override group prioritisation if you are a small organisation, or if you feel you need to show decisive leadership on a specific issue or area.

Back to the plot after my detour into warnings of dire potential pain!

The outcomes we are aiming for in this stage are:

- A set of diagrams that show how we work by drawing up who does what when
- A view of which particular steps cause us problems or are opportunities to improve
- A list of specific actions for us to plan, assign and schedule.

How It Helps The Flow of Purpose

Process Flow is probably the most direct link between our organisation's purpose, and the day to day tasks we do.

The tools in the previous stages have been more about making sure we start from the same baseline, and have the right people involved at the right time. Now, we get those right people asking if each step in our processes could work better, whilst supporting our overall purpose better.

Process Flows starts from the diagrams that you drew in the People & Processes workshop. You will need to organise a group session for each process blob in the People & Processes diagram and go through them in turn. Use your judgement on how much to combine process blobs into the same workshops to minimise the number of workshops to set up.

Who Gets Involved?

For each session you organise, you'll have your ideal list of people by reading around the roles and systems linked to each blob in the related People & Process diagram.

Part Three – The Practicalities

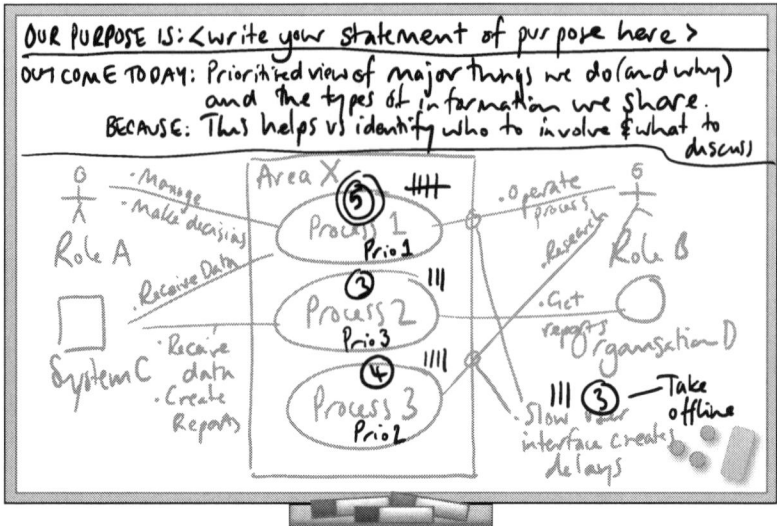

Figure 29 Participants in Process Flow workshops are the Roles (and maybe Systems and Organisations) from the previous tool as repeated here.

So for the area above, if we will be covering all three processes in this workshop, we should invite someone from each of Role A, Role B, System C and someone who deals with Organisation D.

The reality is often that you need to compromise who gets involved in the workshop.

The person who owns the overall Building Block or process may want to be involved, even if they are not directly linked with the process you are looking at. I usually encourage facilitators to accommodate this as it shows good involvement and ownership. It can also help with getting quick decisions on things we can or can't do.

If you have a lot of different roles on your diagram, you may need to pick some individual people that can talk about many roles. Managers or team leaders can be useful here, as can experienced staff members who have held many roles over the years.

For systems listed in the People & Processes diagram, do you have business champions for them, subject matter experts that know the system well, or IT staff who understand how the business uses systems?

In my experience, it's unlikely that you'll want external parties involved; but it's not out of the question. Usually, organisations want to discuss their issues, failings, ideas and possibilities in confidence. However, especially if there is a strong partnership angle to working with a third party, you might want to bring them into process discussions, even if just for a single process. Otherwise, try to invite someone who knows how the relationship with the organisation works.

Using the tool

There is a lot of guidance out there on the internet around the mechanics of using swimlane or cross-functional diagrams. So in The Flow of Purpose, I'll concentrate on sharing my experience of some of the more nuanced parts of taking a group through the diagrams, with purpose.

There are also loads of great software and online tools that help you draw CFDs/swimlanes – try some of them out. If you find they work well in your setting, with your team, they can save a load of time, since you're documenting as you discuss and draw.

As ever, we start by gathering our people together, around a big whiteboard, screen or other way of drawing and noting.

Sometimes, instead of a whiteboard, what works well for Process Flow is to get a page from the flipchart pad, and lay it flat on the table. Then, we can draw our swimlanes directly on it, and use post it notes for process steps, allowing us to move them around until we are happy, and able to draw the links. I'll refer to whiteboard below, but all the steps apply to paper too.

We write at the top of the board (or paper) a reminder of our organisation's statement of purpose, to remind us of our focus.

Then we have our "today's outcomes" and "because" sentences. Work with your group to agree statements along the lines of:

- Our outcome today is a visual map of our X process, showing who does what tasks, how they interlink, and where the opportunities to make improvements might lie
- Because we want to identify specific actions we can take to make our business work better.

With the remaining space on the whiteboard, on the left hand side, write the title or name of every role, organisation or system involved in the process (take these from the People & Processes diagram).

If you can, leave a bit of space to add any roles that we realise we might have forgotten.

Make sure the diagram is labelled as to what process it is exploring. If the process isn't named in your outcome, make sure it's clear in the diagram itself. (Yes, we *should* be able to work it out from what's on the page, but...)

Give each role a "swimlane" across the page by drawing horizontal lines.

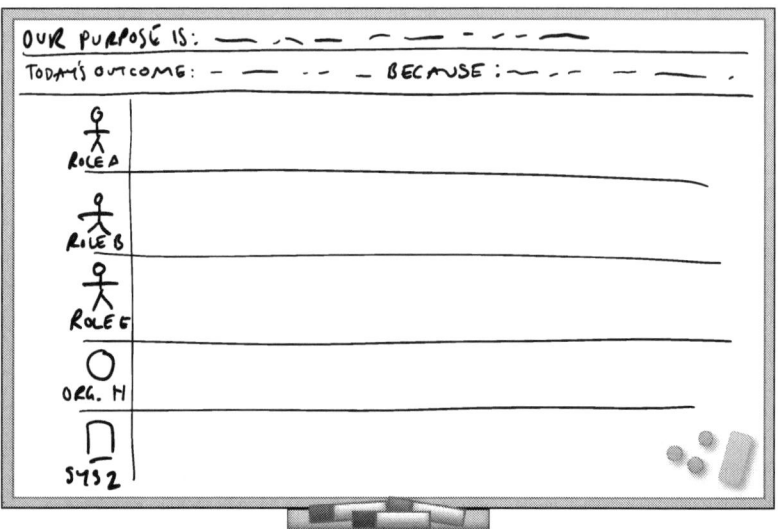

Figure 30 For each process, include each role/other that gets involved

Note, you can also use swimlanes vertically if that suits your needs better – they work just as well. I'll refer to the horizontal arrangement in this section, you can adapt as you need for vertical usage.

Right, we have our framework, let's get analysing.

Think about how the process is initiated – who takes the first step?

A little note here... If I can, I always try to start and end a process with the customer role. Sometimes that's not appropriate, if we're looking at an internal process. However, I always try to link the initiation and conclusion of a process with a customer need (desire) or outcome (trust). Even if it's not

Part Three – The Practicalities

drawn on the diagram, I like to ask people how the customer (and their purpose) fits in to a process. It helps me understand the business better, and it reminds people that customers, our purpose and our processes all go hand in hand.

Anyway, let's say we've had some shout-outs for our first step. Draw that first step in the swimlane for the person who does the task/step – draw up a box with the name of the step in it (or add a post-it with the name in it to the page). The name of the step is a short statement, probably "verb noun" in format. Examples might be "Handle inbound customer call" or "store data in customer record".

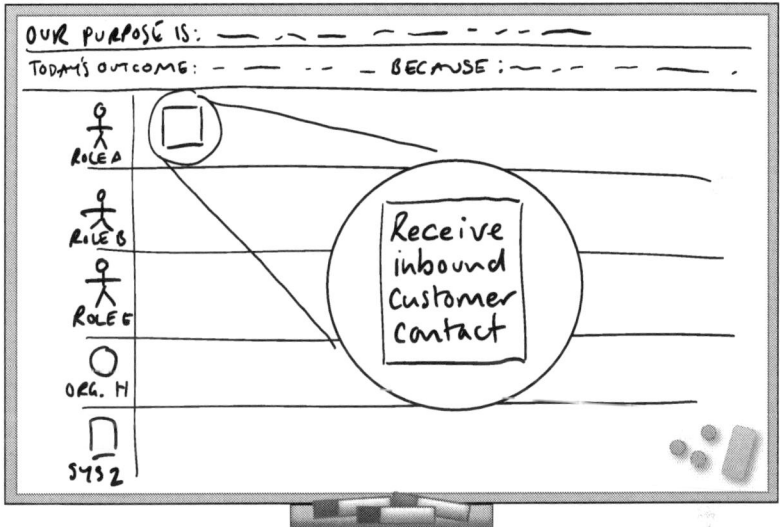

Figure 31 Give each step a short, descriptive title. I've zoomed in here to help.

You can always shuffle, move or amend the step if we find out that the process actually starts a different way, when we think about it a bit more. (Software tools and Post-Its on paper are handy here for shuffling steps vs writing on a whiteboard. If you suspect a lot of shuffling will happen, compromise and stick Post-Its on the whiteboard...)

For every step we draw up, we're basically asking "how does it work now, and what comes next?" What happens next in the current process? What should happen next? What could we do to improve this step? If you come up with ideas or observations for a step, note them down against it. I recommend using a second Post-It to list out your questions, ideas and notes, and hang that post-it off the main step Post-It. I use different colours to keep this clear, yellow Post-Its for steps, and blue Post-Its for notes, or black and blue pens on the whiteboard respectively. (This leaves me the option of using green and pink/red post-its or pens if we need them for positive and negative observations, ideas, notes, etc.). Use whatever flavour of colour-based OCD works for you.

Working left to right, add boxes/Post-Its for subsequent steps, so that the process flows from left to right. Put the box/note in the swimlane of the person who does the step or is accountable for the task. If you're using a whiteboard or software, you may want to draw the connecting lines between steps to show the process flow. On paper, it can be worth holding off on the lines (or use pencil!) as you might need to move or insert steps later.

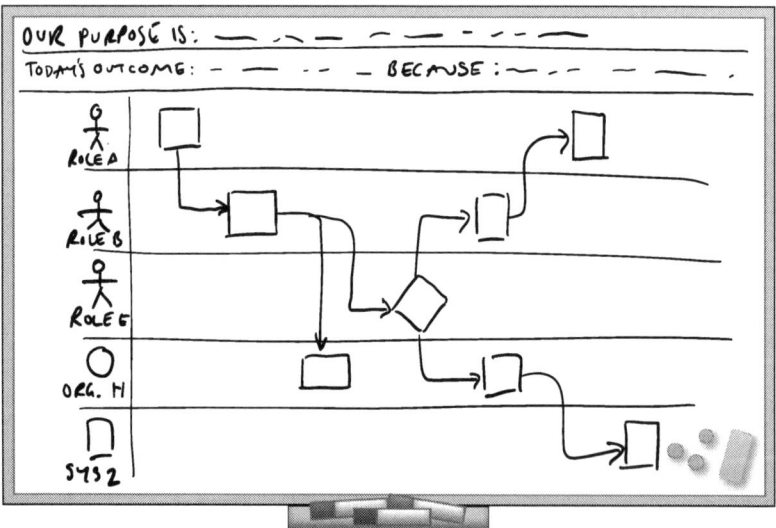

Figure 32 An example of a process flow. Your steps will have names...

If you find that any steps are decisions to be made, rather than actions to be taken, draw them in as diamonds (rhombuses if you want to get technical, or rhombi if you want to get classical). If you're using Post-Its, stick them on at a 45 degree angle. Examples might be "Is this a VIP customer?", "has the performance target been met?" or similar. For each line coming out of the decision rhombus, mark it with the criteria that show why that path would be followed – "yes" or "no" for example.

You'll have to use your judgement on how much to break processes down – i.e. how big should each step be. There are some rules of thumb you can try:

- The more discussion and debate there is about a step, the more you can consider breaking it down. Maybe if you break a big, contentious step down into 3 or 4 smaller steps, it will become clearer where the point of debate is.
- You can think of a step as activity that transforms something in the process. It could be making a decision, gaining a better understanding of something, creating something, changing some information, storing it, or combining/splitting things.

Repeat the actions above until you have explored and documented all the steps in the process.

If you haven't been doing so as you go, draw in the arrows that connect the steps, so you can see the flow through the process.

Now, we should have a diagram which shows all the steps involved in your process, and who does them.

I like to do a sense-check at this stage. Swimlane diagrams might be a bit old school, but they have some really neat benefits. Take each swimlane in turn and follow it across from start to finish. Whilst only looking at that role's steps, the story of the steps should still make sense from that role's point of view.

Part Three – The Practicalities

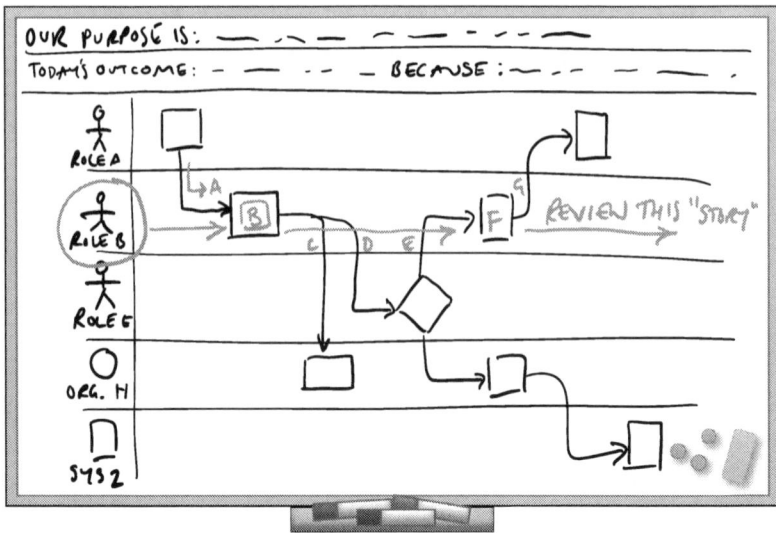

Figure 33 Follow the story of Role B (in glorious grey) through this process

Consider the "story" for Role B in the diagram. I've shown it in grey:

- The first B knows about the process is when they receive information "A" (does that sound right?).
- So they do task B, and pass information C to Organisation H and information D to role E (is that how it works?).
- At some future point, out of the blue comes information E, which leads to task F (does that reflect real life?).
- The last thing Role B does or cares about is passing information G back to Role A (is that it? Anything else happen in reality?).

There should be no surprise appearances of information or responsibilities, and nothing left hanging in the air. Doing this check for each row will often turn up steps that we assumed, missed or have taken for granted. This is usually well worth doing.

What must do now is work out what problems we have where, what causes them, and what we might do to fix them. Or, with a more positive spin, where are our opportunities to simplify, streamline and create more value?

Don't forget in all the brainstorming excitement that we're talking about The Flow of Purpose through our organisation. Try to keep asking if the process steps are helping or hindering our ability to deliver our organisation's overall purpose. It can be all too easy to get sucked into the detail of processes. Sometimes, the question is "given our purpose, should we even be doing this process this way". In other words, if you're going to make things happen right, first make sure they are the right things to do.

There are a number of ways you can approach identifying your problems/opportunities.

The discussions that the group has may already have suggested steps that need to be improved. As a result, you might have *asterisked* or **emboldened** some steps, or filled them with red ink or exclamation marks!!!! (I can turn the irony off now...)

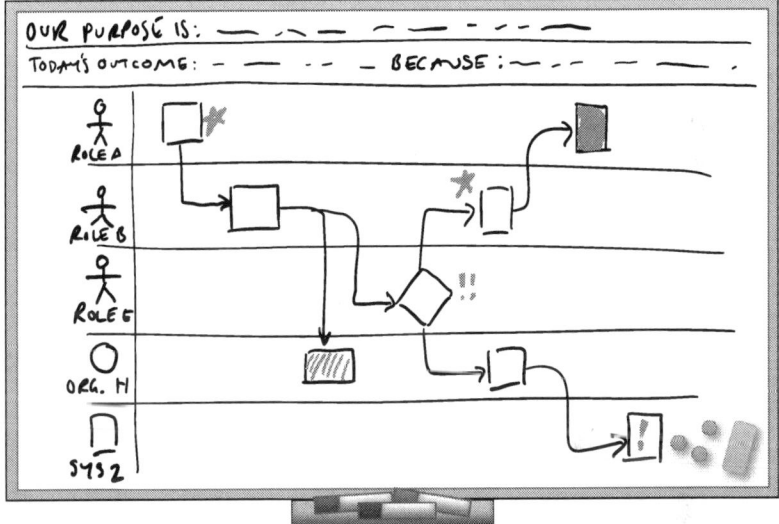

Figure 34 Examples of highlighting steps for exploration or fixing

As well as the ad hoc notes you've made, you could do some quite detailed metrics-based analysis. Work out how many people do each step, how often, with how much effort and elapsed time. You can then look at overall time and effort for the process and look at where these numbers spread through the process steps.

Part Three – The Practicalities

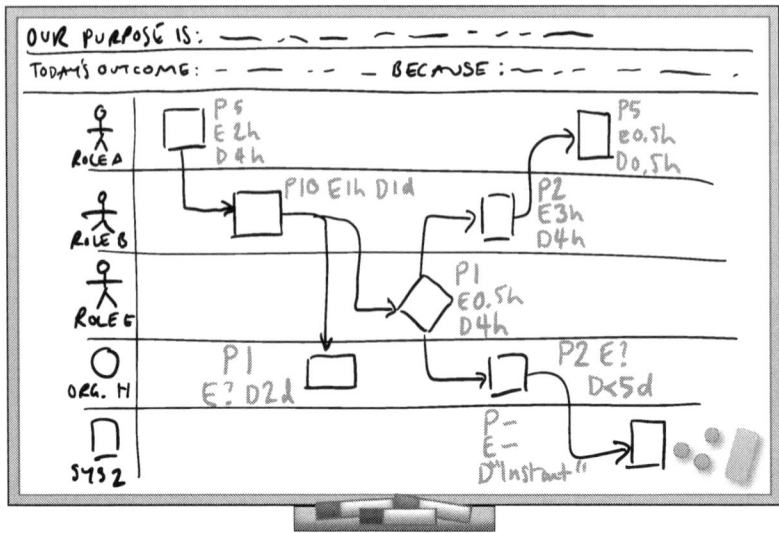

Figure 35 Process steps annotated with metrics

In the diagram above, you can see examples of three metrics; "P" for number of people/organisations, "E" for effort (normally in hours, could be days) and "D" for duration. This lets you multiply up the effort taken for each step, and spot situations where the duration is a lot more than the effort – in other words, there are potential delays. This gives you clues for where to start exploring for improvements.

You could keep things simple, and can do another voting exercise like we've done before, going round the table a few times.

You can use RAG coding – red, amber, green coding. Here, you use a traffic light rating for each box, to show how much it needs to be addressed. You can even decide to have RAG codes for different aspects of each step. For example, you may decide to have three "traffic lights" per step. One might be for how error-prone the step is, another might be for how much it delays the process, and the third might be for how labour-intensive the step is. In this way, by agreeing the three "coloured lights" for each step you can get quite a granular view of quality, delay and effort respectively.

I appreciate the irony of trying to show colour-coding with monochrome printing, but the diagram below should give you the idea…

Part Three – The Practicalities

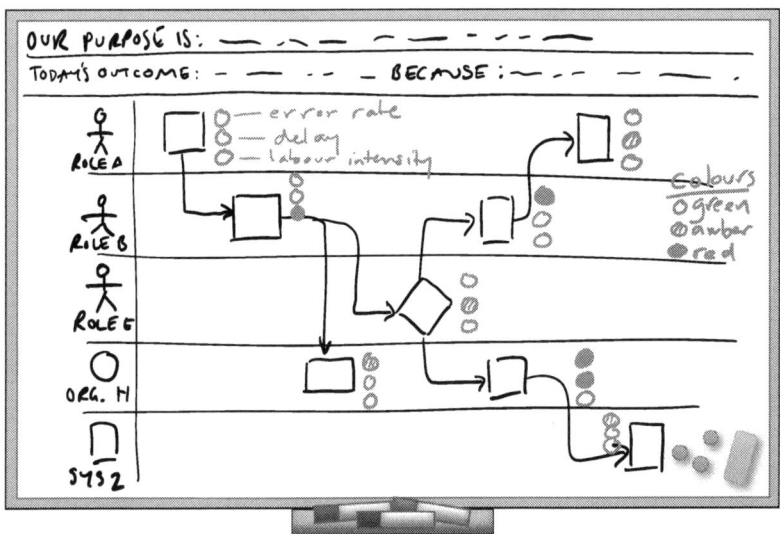

Figure 36 The greyscale version of Red-Amber-Green coding for 3 aspects...

You could use "four box models" (sometimes called Boston Matrices) to score each step in two dimensions, which are often in tension with one another. For example, you might give a high/low position for how mature or proven a step is, versus a high/low score for the step's support for your overall purpose.

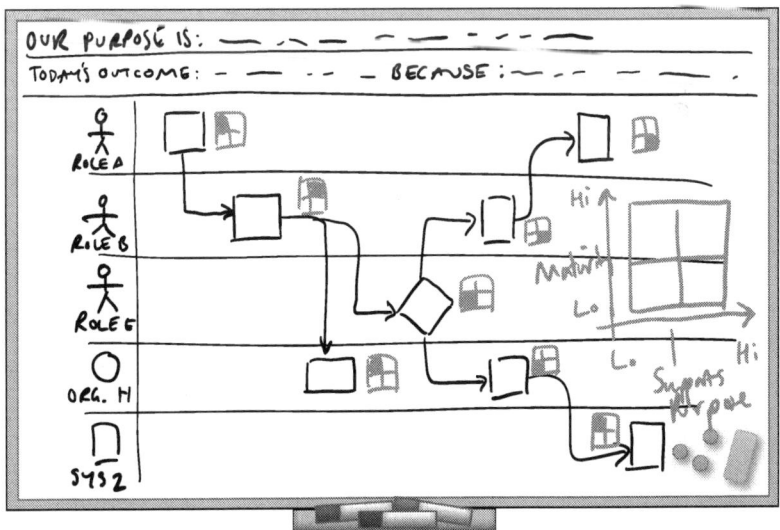

Figure 37 Using a 4-box model to rate and rank steps

Whatever mechanism you use, what we should now be looking at together is a picture of how this process works, with the areas to address clearly identified and labelled.

What To Do With The Outputs

Now we have our process "raw materials", it's time to figure out what we need to do about them. We're going to analyse our process step issues and brainstorm the actions we might take.

I've found that there are a few angles its worth taking when viewing your process for analysis. Here are some ideas for you to try.

Look for Root Causes and Fixes

The most obvious start point is to ask for each "problem step" you've marked, "what is the root cause of this problem?" You might want to use a questioning technique like "The Five Whys" or "fishbone diagram" to help you get to root causes. Search for them online if you haven't come across them before.

If the group can work out the root cause(s) of an issue happening, then we can begin to work out what prevents or controls that root cause. Can we note down beside a step the actions that would solve the problems we identify with that step? These should be real, practical things we can do, start, stop or change.

If we know there's a problem, but we can't see a solution, we may want to create an offline action to explore this one step and possible causes and fixes.

Ownership and Passing Responsibility

A less obvious place to look, but one which is often intriguing, are the points where the process switches into different swimlanes. The way I usually explain this to the groups I work with is that when a process switches lane, responsibility is being passed to another role. It seems pretty obvious put like that. People are usually quite happy with the explanation at this point. However, in a lot of cases, you don't need to delve too much deeper into what this really means to find sources of process problems. I'll often challenge people in the room to think of things like:

- How do we make sure that the new responsible person knows that the job is in their domain now?
- How long handover takes – who feels they're always waiting on whom?
- In what format is information or material passed over?
- What expectations there are of how long the step should take – who's getting grumpy, where/when?
- What feedback or acknowledgement is appropriate to give to the person passing the process on – and why is that so?
- Do we have processes that zig-zag between two lanes?
- How well documented are these handovers – a clue: how do you train new starters to take on these roles?
- How do we track where in the process things are – for a case or instance or whatever, how do we know who it sits with? What do we do if a customer calls in wanting an update on their thing or service or whatever?

Having considered and discussed these, people then tend to be a bit less happy, as these are often hidden root causes for problems. If they've not been considered before, it can feel like fixing these sorts of problems is an intractable challenge. Not so, I believe. Just knowing we face these particular challenges is a great start. Sharing this information with our people and relating the changes we need to make to our organisational purpose will often start to change behaviours and results.

Reordering Steps to Streamline Processes

I want to pick up on those zig-zagging processes. Do you see any swimlanes that appear to be passing information or decisions back and forth between them? If you see this sort of picture, it's a clue that we could streamline our process if we can gather together the information steps and the decision steps. An example of this is, could we collect all the information up front and then make a series of decisions at once, rather than toing-and-froing? Or, can some of the steps be done or decisions be made without passing responsibility – could we train one role to make decisions or do steps that are currently done by the other role?

Do you spot bottlenecks in your processes? Places where things get held up? Steps where the duration is much longer than the effort? Often, these are due to a single person or role being too busy with other priorities. Is that the case here? Or is it down to a dependency – having to wait on someone or something else before the task can be completed?

Depending on what causes the bottleneck, you can consider a few different possible actions to take. You could reprioritise work, so that the step we're looking at gets more time devoted to it. You could employ more people in the role in question.

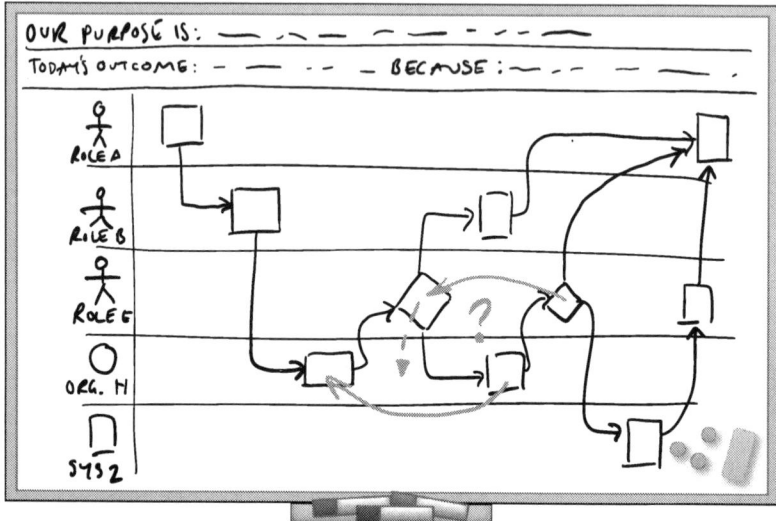

Figure 38 "zig-zagging" processes might be simplified by combining or reassiging steps or decisions

You could look at whether the decision could be made by someone else, perhaps with some training, or systemising the bulk of decisions and only getting your bottleneck person involved in the exceptional cases.

Get creative with brainstorming how a streamlined process might work if we ignored "we've always done it that way" or "that would never work".

Dependencies – When People Are Waiting or Making Others Wait

For dependencies, there are other things to explore. Here are some questions to get you started:

- Is it a true dependency or are we assuming it is – what would happen if we took it out of the picture for this step?
- Does the source of the dependency (the person or thing we're waiting on) know that their output is a dependency?
- Can we change the service level we get from them?
- Can we do the work in a different way, so the dependency has less of an impact?
- Can we let other roles know in advance of the things we need?

When you are facilitating, there are signs to listen and look for, which suggest there are dependencies. Are people discussing how we are always waiting on something (information or materials) before we can move ahead with a step? Look also for scenarios where people are discussing how they always feel they are being chased for things? They may feel that they are busy, and people chasing them are just a hassle – but those chasers might be a sign of a subsequent step being dependent on the one we're looking at now.

If you find a dependency, show it as such on your diagram – the easiest way is just to label the line between steps with the note "dependency". Sometimes, the underlying dependency might affect a few steps – feel free to draw that in as a specific dependency line or arrow – anything that makes it clear in your diagram.

Part Three – The Practicalities

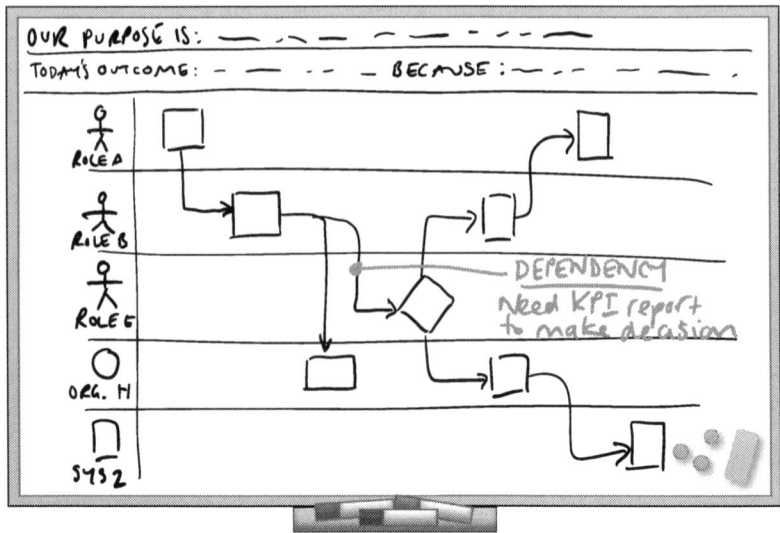

Figure 39 Highlighting specific dependencies

What if you find a dependency?

Well, the root cause and streamlining sections above actually give you some pretty good tools to explore dependencies. After all, dependencies are caused by something, and need some change to fix them.

Often, just pointing out to the people involved that they are at either end of a dependency will start the ideas flowing.

One word of warning – I've found that sensitive facilitation can be needed around dependencies as it is very easy for people to become either accusatory or defensive. After all, we are exploring things that delay, impact or let down others. If the people discussing their interdependency have been involved in The Flow of Purpose work so far, you should find that they are approaching the discussion in a positive and purpose-driven way, since we've been through sharing purpose. Still, it's worth being prepared for bruised egos or little interpersonal issues.

Are You Spotting Patterns?

With the next tool (Purpose Driven Plans), we'll be gathering fixes and actions into groups. For now, whilst you have your group together, it is worth

Part Three – The Practicalities

asking them at this stage whether they feel there are some themes or natural groupings emerging.

If we look at the problems and opportunities we are uncovering in our diagram, can we group the actions into themes, driven by the overall purpose? If we can then perhaps indicate this on the diagram.

Examples of these trends or patterns that I've seen in work I've done over the years include things like:

- Changing culture
- Improving communications
- Delivering our strategy
- Getting the best people on board
- Right first time.

I'm sure you can think of many others. If you can, drive your themes from your organisation's statement of purpose. At least find a way to link the themes with working more to your purpose.

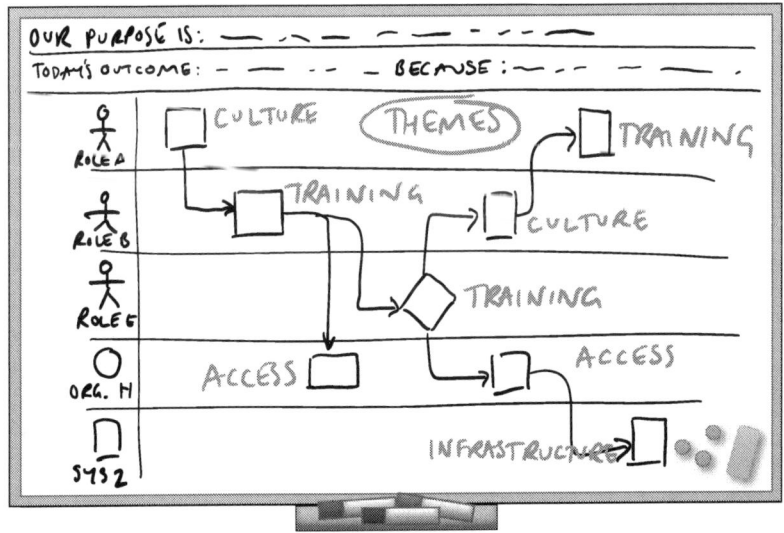

Figure 40 Collecting steps (and therefore issues & fixes) into themes

Don't worry about finessing titles or reducing the number of themes just now. We'll do that with the next tool. At the moment, we're just looking to use the group's input to build us a long-list of potential themes so we're not starting the next stage from a blank sheet of paper.

Swimlanes As a Basis For Further Work

As Process Flows is based on swimlanes, a fairly general analysis tool, it won't surprise you to know that I've seen the diagrams we create used in many ways beyond The Flow of Purpose. Here are some ideas for you.

Group Analysis

You can approach Process Flows as a group exercise rather than one big workshop. This works especially well with paper and Post-Its. Instead of having one diagram that everyone debates and which you annotate, split people into smaller groups. Give each group a big pad of paper and a stock of Post-Its (and pens, if you want to get pedantic). Then help each group work on processes independently. If each group looks at the same process, you could have different viewpoints on it to generate ideas and find issues. If you want to cover a lot in a short period of time, have different groups analyse different processes. Either way, have each group give a short presentation to the workshop on their diagrams, questions and conclusions (to boost communication and help avoid the risk of missing obvious things by splitting the work).

Use with Agile

Because we can get straight from the diagram the role, task and context, it is fairly straightforward to define user stories for Agile projects and development. What's doubly useful is that you already start from having some view of priority. That helps to work out where in the project cycle stories should be – in development or in the backlog. This also gives you a chance to sanity check whether the analysis and Agile priorities agree. If not, why did we see things differently? It's not a question of who's right and who's wrong, rather, what can we learn from each other?

Service Design

With some thoughtful layout, you can get a clear view of the customers and suppliers for a service. This can help you with service design. Here's an idea to get you started. Collect your "customer side" roles at the top of the diagram. Gather your supplier or external roles at the bottom of the diagram. In the middle, put your "service provision" roles. Treat these middle roles as

Part Three – The Practicalities

something of a black box – you know (and explore/define) what happens in there, but your suppliers and customers don't, so you need to think clearly about the "touch-points," "interfaces" or "customer experience" depending on how you want to put it.

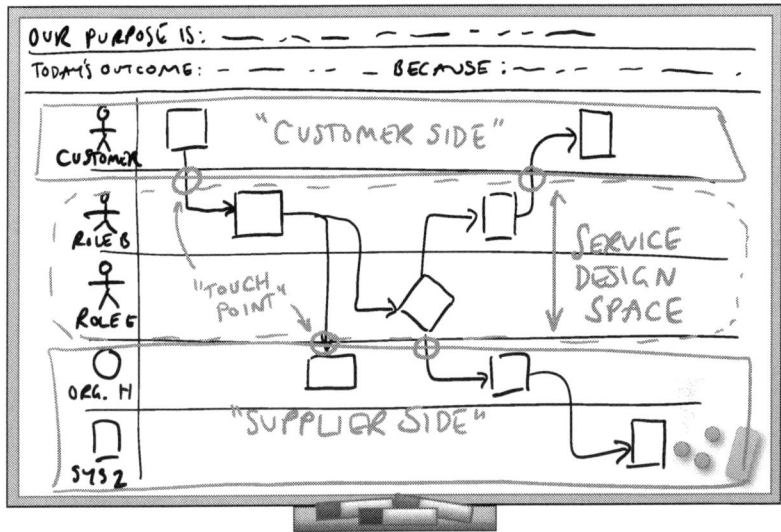

Figure 41 Using swimlanes to support Service Design

I view design as being "creation with purpose", so you can see how having our purpose and outcomes as the context for our diagram, plus a clear boundary around our service, helps us to explore and debate the purpose and design of our services, not just our processes, at a high level.

Visual Job Descriptions

Hands up who regularly reads the wording of their job description to make sure they are doing the right things and keeping the right people informed?

OK, I know some will, especially in very demanding, compliance-driven or life-and-death type roles. But come on now, be honest...

I've been doing some intriguing work lately, on using the Process Flow diagrams to build visual job descriptions.

Look at it this way. We've looked at the main processes across our business, and broken them down into sets of stories – remember how we sanity checked our processes by "reading" each role from left to right? Well, for a given role, if you pulled together each one of these stories from across all the diagrams, you'd have a pictorial view of the tasks a given role gets involved in. In other words, extract all their "lanes" from the diagrams, and you now have a visual job description.

To really make this fly, whenever the "process arrow" enters "my" role's swimlane, we say who passed the process on to me, and what info (and responsibility came with it). Similarly, on my "outbound arrows", we can note who gets my output, and what information, material or responsibility that is. To keep everything pulling along together, remember we can recap our corporate purpose at the top of the document – our big why.

People often understand pictures quicker than lists and wordy paragraphs. So if we want people to truly understand how their role delivers our purpose, what better way than pictures? How much easier to gather people together for a quick ad-hoc session on "how do we improve how we work?" when your start point is an analysis diagram!

What next?

As you've read, there is quite a lot you can do with the outputs of the Process Flows tool.

In The Flow of Purpose, the next step is to draw up your purpose driven plans. This is where we turn the ideas and analysis into actionable plans, in a way that helps create buy-in across our organisations.

The most important thing to do now, is to make sure that you have a single list of the actions you have identified through the Process Flows for the current Building Block area. These are the actions the groups identified that will address root causes of problems. The next tool takes these actions and puts them in a structured plan.

A plan which shows people why every task and action matters.

Part Three – The Practicalities

Part Three – The Practicalities

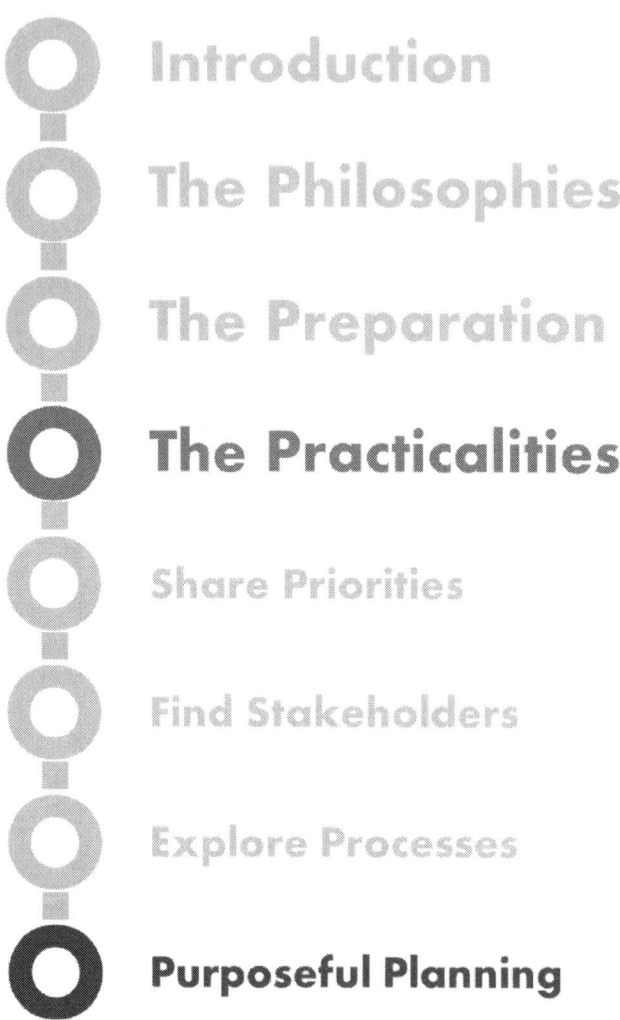

Introduction

The Philosophies

The Preparation

The Practicalities

Share Priorities

Find Stakeholders

Explore Processes

Purposeful Planning

Part Three – The Practicalities

18 Purposeful Planning

What Is It?

A Purpose Driven Plan is a form of action planning that connects people's actions, through flows of purpose, to us delivering our overall outcomes and purpose. It's actually where the title The Flow of Purpose came from.

Many plans are either lists or Gantt charts, or variants of these like Kanban boards (like Trello.com).

Purpose Driven Plans take a slightly different approach to planning out the action we need to take.

They're a visual way of showing how tasks and actions relate to the purpose of improvements and change.

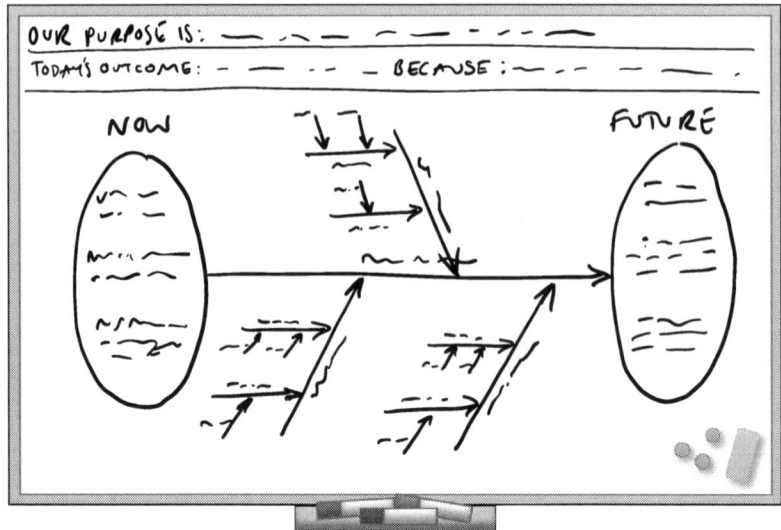

Figure 42 A Purpose Driven Plan shows our journey to a better future with the contributing statements of purpose – The Flow of Purpose

Why Use it? Purpose & Outcomes

The main reason for using Purpose Driven Plans is actually the need for motivating people through change.

Why? Taking action means doing something differently. Either once, to change a situation, or repeatedly to adopt a new way of doing things.

Either way, we're talking about change.

And what tends to create friction, delay and upset in organisations?

Change.

So my reasoning was, if change threatens great action and outcomes, then planning must acknowledge the need to deal with change.

How do we deal with change?

I think it's about desire and trust again. We need people to believe that the change is needed and trust that the outcomes will be better.

I wanted to find a way to get people not just to take on tasks as part of my plans, but to believe in them. If people believe in their work, they overcome the momentum, friction, pain, setbacks and time demands that otherwise turn great ideas into failed initiatives.

I had to find a way to connect individual actions with our overall purpose.

I needed something that complemented existing planning tools used in my clients, by adding a valuable layer on top that was all about the "why" of tasks – something that many other approaches don't include.

It was this sort of dilemma that made me think and design and try and test Purpose Driven Plans.

How It Helps The Flow of Purpose

Within The Flow of Purpose, the Purpose Driven Plan is the bridge between the analysis and the results.

Especially in the Process Flows (swimlanes) diagram, we will have noted down a load of root causes and potential fixes. There will be some small things to do, and some large undertakings. There will be clear tasks and hazier improvements. We may have a load of possible themes that have suggested themselves through the work. Above all, we will have a load of things to explore, do and achieve, which are driven by our organisation's statement of purpose.

What we need to do now is put the actions we identify into a document that shows what's being done and why.

Optionally, we can include in the Purpose Driven Plan who owns each action, when it needs to be done by, and the priority. Why do I say this is optional? If we already have a project or action management approach, then use that – don't force people to learn something new if they don't need to. Purpose Driven Plans are still useful in explaining the *purpose* for tasks within other planning systems.

Why does all this matter?

It comes back to motivation through change. We want to make it easy for people to remind themselves why it is worth persevering with change. To stick with it when they are busy, demotivated, sceptical or cynical or just tired and in need of an easy day.

Part Three – The Practicalities

Who Gets Involved?

There are two ways to answer this. First, who do you involve in creating the plan? Second, who appears in the plan (as named owners of tasks/actions)?

On the first question, we can usually work with quite a small group (maybe even on our own). We're looking for the core of people who know how action gets taken across your business or organisation. People with authority to make decisions and direct staff and effort. A good start point is the leadership group we discussed way back at the start of Part Three when we covered defining your organisation's statement of purpose. (we can always iterate through the plan and delegate out "arms" of it to people to include more details). Look at the areas where action is needed. Are there senior managers, leaders or experienced staff that can or need to get things done in their broad areas? Consider including them in your planning session.

For the second question, the glib answer is "everyone who has an action". Taken to its furthest degree, if a tasks needs to be done by an identified individual, we can note their name against the task. Sometimes however, it makes more sense to assign such tasks to an overall accountable person. Then they can decide which individual does the task – we balance accountability against over-planning that way.

To help us navigate this question – how do we currently manage our planned work? Individual tasks, or overall accountability? And how does that work? Well enough to stick with it, or is there a case for trying the opposite approach? How could we test and measure whether more or less detail will give you better results?

Use your judgement and common sense for both these questions...

There is a third angle on involvement too: communication.

Purpose Driven Plans are also a good way of communicating what we are seeking to do (and why, obviously) and how we are getting on once we're under way.

The wider business tends to appreciate the visual message that "we started here, we're heading there because of our purpose, and to achieve that we need to do these things".

It also lays clear the case for taking action. These are not just random changes that we are throwing at people. They are part of a coherent, bigger

Part Three – The Practicalities

picture. People sometimes don't see beyond their role or team, so impacts upon them, shown within a wider context, can be quite powerful.

Using the tool

As with all the tools, we start by writing our organisation's purpose at the top of the whiteboard. This keeps our thinking on track towards the ultimate end game.

Below that we write our outcomes and because sentences. These keep our minds focused on what we need to produce as a result of this session, and why it matters. You might have statements like:

- Our outcome today is a visual plan of action that shows why each task or action matters
- Because an understanding of how individual tasks fit with our purpose helps to motivate people

To start our plan proper, we begin with a current state and a future state. Draw up two blobs at either end of the whiteboard, with an arrow connecting them. Label the left hand blob "Now" and the right hand blob "Future".

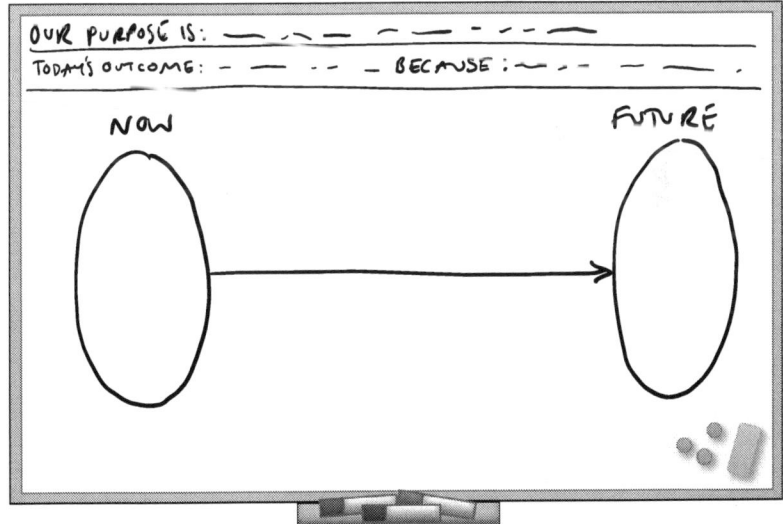

Figure 43 Starting your Purpose Driven Plan

Our next step is to write a few pithy lines in each blob that help us show how our state will change by taking these actions. It should be high level, but be challenging, compelling and believable.

It's worth spending a bit of time on getting these just right. They "bookend" the plan. The ideal situation for our needs is that the "now" should feel costly and untenable, and the "future" should feel achievable and rewarding. Incidentally, I know that's quite an emotive way of putting it. Thinking of it in these terms gives as a final check point. If the start and end points don't genuinely feel like this, then why are we doing the analysis and planning exercise in the first place – have we missed something?

Let's assume we're confident that we need to move on in future. How do we go about writing the now and future statements?

Obviously that's a very difficult question to answer in a book, because it will be utterly dependent on your circumstances. There is no magic formula to share here. What I will do is share with you the kind of thought process I use when I'm consulting with clients. You have your experience of using the earlier tools, the inputs from your colleagues, and your overall statement of purpose. With a bit of thinking and discussion, I'm confident you'll end up with a great set of end points to bookend your plan.

Here are some questions to consider and some ideas to try:

Look at the way your organisation's statement of purpose is structured. Could you break it down into a few elements that work together to create the overall purpose? If so, then you could say for each of those elements, where are we now, and how do we want it to be in the future?

If you had to pick 2 or 3 headings to describe what changes you are trying to achieve, what would those headings be? Considering this could help you write your short summaries of now and the future. Where are you and where do you want to be with each of those headings?

You may have a collection of suggested themes from the Process Flows work you did in the previous step. I know this is getting a bit "meta", but do the themes feel like they fit into a few broad groupings? If you spot these "meta-themes" for your root cause fixes and actions, can you write your now/future states in those terms?

Part Three – The Practicalities

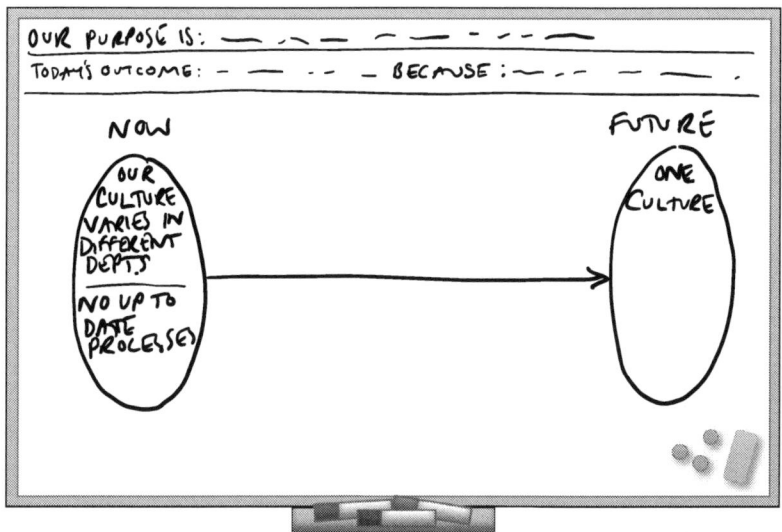

Figure 44 Starting to identify elements of our current & future states

It might be that you are really struggling to think about how to put your now/future statements (or perhaps there is a lot of debate that is going nowhere). My fall back in these circumstances is to turn to my Nine Word Business Model. Have a look under the "Set Your Purpose & Strategy" section if you want a reminder of the details of the words and what they mean.

To use them, you can run through each of the words in turn, perhaps explaining a little about what they mean in your organisation's context. For each of the nine words, ask people whether they feel we could improve on how we currently do it. Score the need for improvement from 1-5 or 1-10 or whatever. Pick the top 2-4 areas (the ones that need the most improvement, in most people's eyes). Now, write down how well we deal with each area now, and what it needs to change to in the future.

I've mentioned 2 or 3 headings for each of the blobs – but don't let that constrain you if you feel there are 4 or 5 or even 10. Use your judgement as to how much to summarise things into fewer headings, versus breaking down into more. Fewer headings makes it easier to communicate and spread the word (less to grasp immediately), but more headings help to illustrate the scale and scope of the challenges and opportunities we face.

Whatever approach you use, come up with now and future statements that you believe in.

We now need to write up the specific purpose for the programme of work we are planning. We start by considering your organisation's purpose (top of whiteboard), and the now-to-future changes we have just written up (blobs). We must write along the arrow what the purpose of the programme is.

In other words, what sentence can we write that justifies why we need to change the now state to be the future state?

This may well be different to your organisation's overall purpose. Usually the purpose on the now-to-future arrow is about changes we'll make as an organisation (as opposed to changes we make to our customers' lives). But the two purposes should feel consistent. Does it sound like achieving our now-to-future purpose will make us more able to deliver our overall purpose? Hopefully, yes. If not, it's not game over, but perhaps try to think what the link might be. Maybe you need to stop doing something as an organisation, before you can properly move forward.

Here's how it should end up looking at this stage.

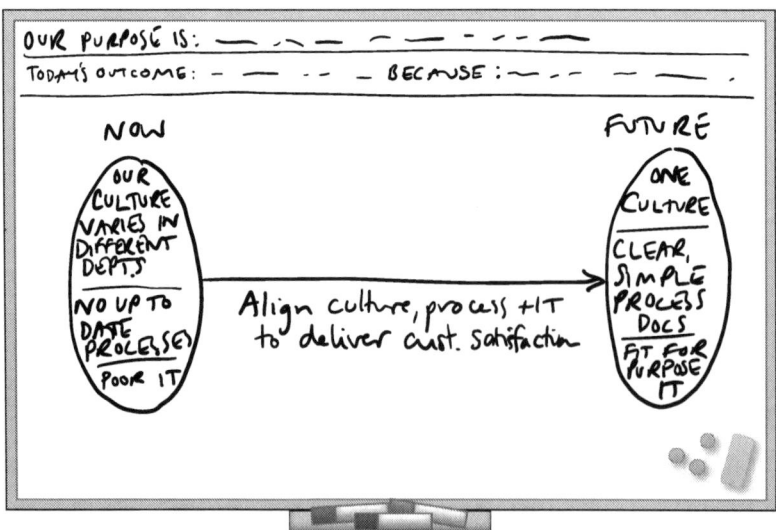

Figure 45 Statements of Now and Future, connected with a Purpose - why we must make these changes

What we do next is draw in the supporting themes or areas that feed into delivering this main purpose and outcome. If you've ever done a root cause analysis diagram (sometimes called a fishbone diagram) then you will have done something similar.

In a root cause analysis diagram, you start with a problem, and keep asking "why does that happen" in a structured way, until you have dug right down to the underlying root cause(s) of the problem.

In a purpose driven plan we ask instead "what change or transformation will enable this?" When we have our answers, we draw in new arrows, with those answers, in support of the main purpose.

Here's what that looks like in practice.

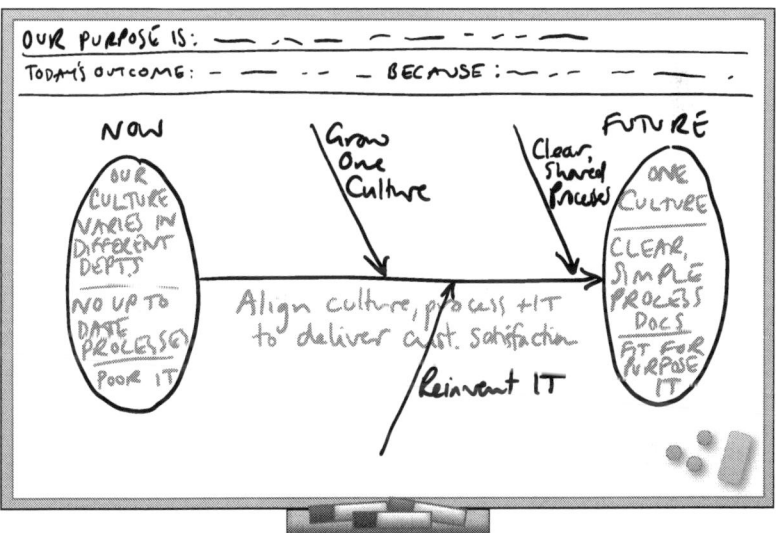

Figure 46 Adding some major contributing transformations - "helping whys"

In this example, we have a main purpose of:

- "Align culture, process and IT to deliver customer satisfaction".

There are three supporting or contributing purposes/transformations:

- "Grow one culture"
- "Clear, shared processes" and
- "Reinvent IT".

I usually aim for about 3-8 contributing arrows, but use as many or as few as you need – if in doubt, note that we'll break each one down further, so you don't need to get too detailed yet.

Sometimes, I'll work with the group to define an "above the line" and "below the line" meaning, if that helps us with planning and communication. An example of this might be that one off transformations of how we operate might be on the arrows above the main purpose, and improvements to business-as-usual might go on the arrows below the line. In this case, the location of the arrows helps people to understand and explain which are major changes and which are new habits, and so need different mind-sets, possibly even different types of people working on them.

Other examples of above/below the line could be customer facing vs internal activities, or creative vs operational, or engineering vs sales, and so on. Use whatever split suits your purposes.

What we now have is a top level view of how purpose flows through major changes and change enablers (contributing arrows).

Who's Responsible?

At this point, it can be useful to debate and agree who will be accountable for each of the contributing arrows.

By putting a name or initials against each arrow, we are saying that this person will be held to account for the delivery of this area of purpose. They make the decisions, they organise the effort, they manage the results in order to deliver the specific area of purpose. By reviewing the names against the contributing arrows, we all understand how we and our colleagues will be contributing to the overall purpose and success. This helps us to work together, support one another and warn one another if we think our work might impact on someone else's purpose. Decision making, delegation, management, reporting and communications are all helped if you can assign clear accountability for areas of purpose, and keep people communicating and collaborating.

Part Three – The Practicalities

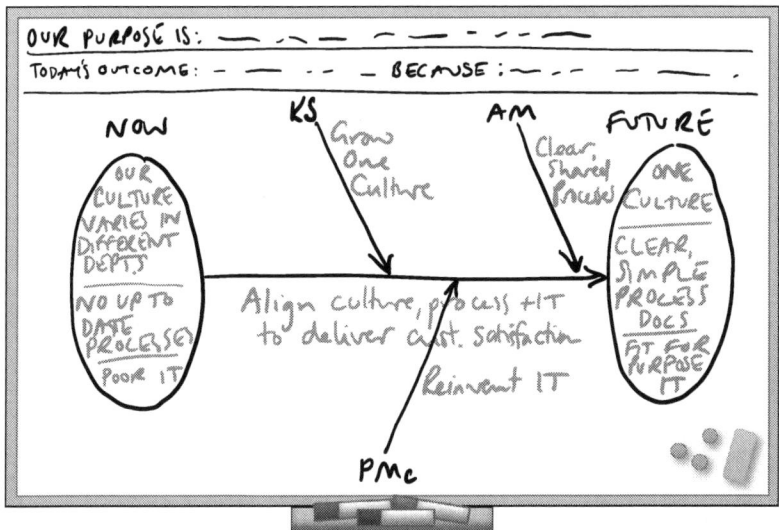

Figure 47 Adding owners' initials or names to make accountability clear.

We can move to the next level without setting accountability here, but the risk is that accountability for actions end up scattered across different contributing arrows. This can happen particularly if we have cross-functional teams, or are working on projects that need lots of teams to work together. Because purpose rises above team boundaries, this can leave us facing a sort of "matrix management".

If we feel this could cause an issue in our organisation, we have a couple of options. We can use purpose to change the way we work, or we can rejig the arrows to more closely match our organisation. To change the way we work is a more strategic option; but if we get buy-in from people through creating the Purpose Driven Plan, why not give it a go? Otherwise, to rejig responsibilities, have a look at our contributing arrows again. Can we split, combine, or otherwise change the arrows to align more with business units or existing senior decision maker roles?

It's more important to be pragmatic about getting projects working towards delivering purpose, than to be dogmatic about applying a rigid model.

Break Down And Iterate

As I mentioned earlier, in a Purpose Driven Plan, our constant question is "what change or transformation will enable this?"

We take each of the contributing arrows, with its purpose, and ask ourselves "what change or transformation will enable this?" When we come up with projects or major activities that will support the purpose in question, we write those down as horizontal arrows. Note against them what the project or activity is, along with its own contributing purpose – a word or two on why it matters. I often use different coloured pens for project/activity name, purpose/why and other data.

We can also add against the project or activity things like owner, priority and by-when date, if that's easy to identify. Otherwise, we can add these data in later, when we turn The Flow of Purpose view into an actual plan.

By doing this exercise until we run out of projects or activities to add, we should end up with something like this "Reinvent IT" example (albeit yours will probably have loads more detail on it):

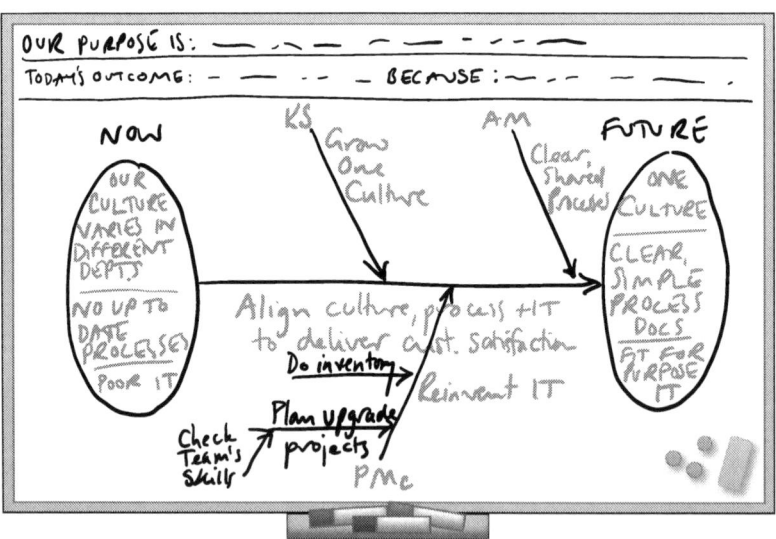

Figure 48 Iterate and add in supporting changes to a suitable level

Now, we can keep iterating to finer levels of detail until we run out of actions to add, or feel we are getting into too much detail to plan.

Taking each horizontal project or activity arrow in turn, ask what actions would need to be done, why. Draw these in as smaller contributing arrows, with an activity name and purpose/why.

Once more, we can assign an owner, priority and date if that seems sensible, or will provoke useful debate.

At this point in The Flow of Purpose process, we'll have a team that are pretty engaged with why we need to change. They'll probably have some great ideas about what we need to fix or start/stop doing. Remember also that we'll also probably have a good stock of ideas, fixes and questions that have arisen through the earlier stages. We review our "take offline" notes to remind ourselves of what the groups identified.

The Purpose Driven Plan is the point where we pull together all these requirements, fixes and actions. Aim to put the actions and fixes on an appropriate arrow within the Plan. It might be that when we come to place actions on the plan, we need to modify or add arrows. That's OK, as long as all the purposes still fit the overall picture.

We might feel that we need to modify or add an arrow and something then seems out of place. That's a sign that there may be a mismatch of purposes. Are some actions or arrows now inconsistent with the main purpose connecting our current and future states? Does it feel like something has been missed when we set our main purpose? Sometimes, when we go through The Flow of Purpose process, we uncover things that weren't apparent when we started and set our initial statement of purpose. If the gap is major, you may want to go back to one of the earlier stages in The Flow of Purpose, to re-examine one or more areas. This will let us incorporate what we have learnt into updated outcomes and documents.

We're now getting quite detailed in the planning exercise. At this stage, I'll often explain to the group that we are doing a first pass of the planning, but that we probably need more input from others to finish the plan. This is where having people accountable for each main arrow helps, because they can each take their arrow away to break down further. Then we can reconvene and draw up our detailed map.

Regardless of whether we do the plan in one sitting, or delegate out the detail, we should end up with something that looks like this:

Part Three – The Practicalities

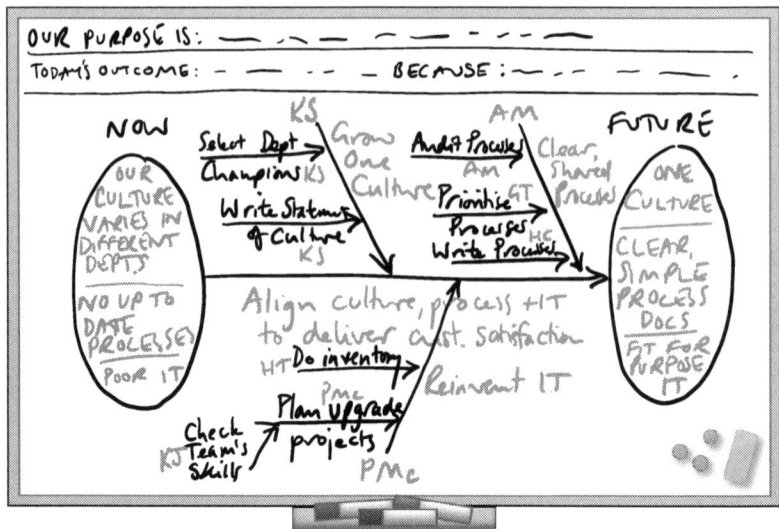

Figure 49 A Purpose Driven Plan, with actions/owners shown - you may have much more detail...

At first glance, it can look a bit busy, but there is a lot of useful information in this diagram.

We end up with a map of actions with purpose that cascade down to the main purpose, so any given person responsible for a task "gets" why their work is important in the big picture. By giving people access to the overall Purpose Driven Plan, they can follow their own story – from their action down through all the things it contributes to, to the main reason we are all doing all of this stuff.

"I do this because... because... because, which all matters because..." until you get to the main purpose and transformation at the heart of the Purpose Driven Plan.

That's another crucial angle to Purpose Driven Plans – not only can I see my story – but I can trace the story of everyone else in the picture too. That's a recipe for us really valuing the contribution we all make, even if we don't fully understand other's roles.

My experience is that this type of understanding and valuing is really beneficial at times of great change. Many people's natural inclination through change is to home in on their own circumstances, perhaps feeling that they alone are shouldering an unfair share of the burden and everyone else gets it easy. Or occasionally people feel that they are getting away lightly and some other sucker is taking the pain... One of those outlooks tends to be more common than the other! Anyway, the point is that Purpose Driven Plans illustrate to people just how much is involved in doing things that matter. They can even foster a more collaborative approach, where people look for opportunities to help, support and advise others.

Other Things To Try

When you are confident using the approach, another little finessing technique we can use is to write the task arrows in priority or time order. First, agree our ordering scheme – is it priority or time, and is it first/highest at the inner or outer end of the arrow? Then decide where on the arrow each task goes – then we get a really nice visual effect as tasks are completed "down the line". This also helps us very quickly spot tasks which have not been done on time or in priority order. So, this is not just a way of prettifying the diagram, but helps with risk identification and management.

Since they're very visual, I've also found that Purpose Driven Plans provide a good home for RAG (Red Amber Green) coding of things like risk, effort or duration. Rather than hiding your risk log away in a folder somewhere (where most risk logs live, it seems), we can keep risk at the forefront of thinking and planning. Use a red dot, or triangle, or whatever metaphor works in our organisation, to rate each area, project or task as high (red), medium (amber) or low (green) risk. Or do the same for effort. Or use two symbols to let us use RAG coding for multiple parameters. Just make sure we have a key that explains what everything means when someone views the plan.

What To Do With The Outputs

In some ways, the Purpose Driven Plan is used like any other plan. It should be shared and communicated, and progress should be reviewed regularly.

Visio, Draw.io or similar diagramming software is an ideal way to formally draw up & share your Purpose Driven Plan. Even PowerPoint or Keynote can work. If you want to build on a template to save time, look for a "Root Cause Analysis" or "Fishbone Diagram" template.

Ownership

The first part of using the plan is to make sure that all activities have owners – or that we will assign owners as time goes on. We need to make sure that the owners know that they have these tasks, and how (and why) they can read The Flow of Purpose through the Purpose Driven Plan. Task owners who have not been involved in The Flow of Purpose process may be sceptical, so do take some time to sell the concept to them if needed. Make sure any key dates have been shared and are shown on the plan.

Communication

The next thing Purpose Driven Plans are good for is communicating programmes more widely. If we have a version of our plan where detail is streamlined down to action/project names and purposes (i.e. not things like priorities and RAG coding), it will be very clear to a wider audience how there is a "why" for everything we need to do. They can see how purpose flows through our activities, to deliver change.

We can simply share or project on-screen the Purpose Driven Plan in its entirety, and pick sections to explain. If we want to invest a bit more time, we can do things like building the plan on-screen through the different levels of "arrow". This lets us show how the big purpose is enabled by contributing purposes and projects, and how they in turn are supported by purposeful actions.

Tracking & Managing Progress

Having a plan that people have bought into is good, but to make most use of the work we have done, we'll want to actively manage the activities we identified.

I suggest setting up a regular plan review session – pick a cadence that suits the organisation, but weekly, fortnightly or monthly are the most usual. Occasionally daily reviews work for short or risky projects, or quarterly for long term projects. We can even arrange reviews at different frequencies for parts of the plan. For example, each accountable person could review their contributing arrow and its constituent actions weekly with team members, with the main plan being reviewed monthly by the "accountables".

Part Three – The Practicalities

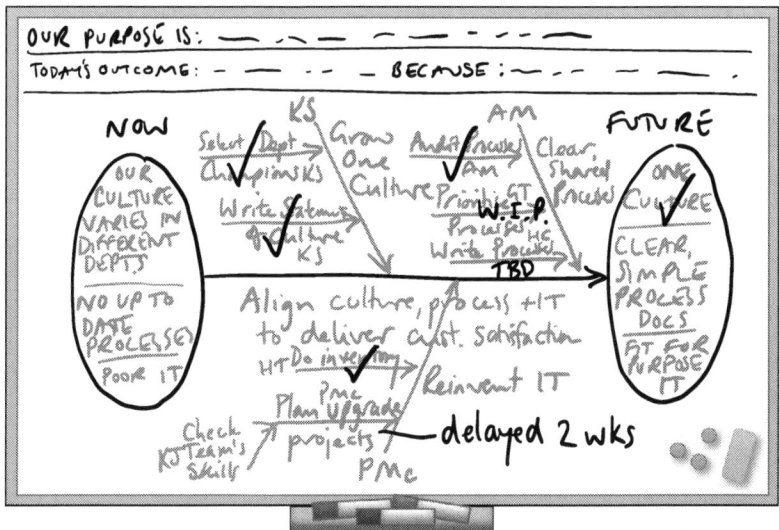

Figure 50 A very simple way of showing progress through the plan

At first glance, the Purpose Driven Plan doesn't have the clear time illustrating component of a Gantt chart plan. However, we can get an element of this by ordering your tasks by time down the arrows – as explained in the "Other Things To Try" section.

What if we already have an established planning approach in use; maybe Gantt charts, backlogs for Agile working, to-do lists, or similar?

No problem, these can all work well with the Purpose Driven Plans. The trick is to keep the Purpose Driven Plan at a high level and put the details in your established method. In this case, the Purpose Driven Plan becomes more of a high-level map that shows The Flow of Purpose that links to the detailed plans. Our Purpose Driven Plan is much more likely to focus on outcomes (and why they matter) than specific activities. When doing our project reviews, prior to going through our established tools, we can have a quick recap of the Purpose Driven Plan to make sure that all our projects still feel like they are delivering to purpose, before digging into task details.

What next?

If you've got to this stage for the first time, using The Flow of Purpose, then you're probably working through the actions in your first priority area.

(Remember the Six Building Blocks of Business? This was when you set your broad priorities.)

Now it's time to go through The Flow of Purpose process for the second (or subsequent) priority area (you can debate whether it's still the next priority if you need to). It's now time to analyse, dig into people and process, find root causes and fixes and make Purpose Driven Plans, in a new area.

There can be a temptation at this point to keep going with the momentum you've built in the first area. That's perfectly valid – but only if it's the right thing to do… If you have different owners for each of your Building Blocks, they may well feel aggrieved that their priority is being pushed further back, if you keep going with further analysis of the first priority area. If the group agrees to stick with the top priority area, then go for it. Otherwise, decide when it make sense to come back to the initial area. In other words, re-prioritise extending or finishing the current along with the existing other areas.

A Call To Action

19 Start Your Flow of Purpose

We started on this journey by saying that The Flow of Purpose is the way we make everything we do in our business meaningful:

> *The Flow of Purpose is the way we make every business action meaningful to people, by linking it with a core, driving purpose that crosses over job or departmental boundaries.*
>
> *With a flow of purpose, everything we do in our business has meaning. To us, to the people later in the process, to the people who passed the task on to us, to our colleagues and to our customers.*
>
> *Everyone is playing a part in something that matters. We're all making changes and improvement that matter.* **The Flow of Purpose is about finding that purpose, that meaning, getting it as clear as it can be, and getting people to buy in to it.**
>
> *When do we know we have a flow of purpose through our organisation? When we ask people in any role "why do we do things this way?" and we get the same compelling answer from everyone.*

A Call To Action

In the three parts of The Flow of Purpose, I hope I have shared with you some ideas, questions and tools that you find useful. You can use them to find your organisation's purpose, express it clearly, and show people how purpose makes our tasks, activities and projects matter and make a difference.

The Flow of Purpose is a dynamic thing. It's engaging and lively and visual and iterative. The discussion it promotes both challenges and enlightens people. But it needs to be nurtured. You need to feed it with time and care in the early days. You need to keep the purpose flowing with regular reviews and revisits. Don't let the great work you do fade on a whiteboard or gather dust in a folder.

The most important thing now is to start your own Flow of Purpose:

The wilful and coordinated sharing of reasons and determination to do things that create advantage

Good luck! I'd love to hear how you get on...

KS.

hello@theflowofpurpose.com

Printed in Great Britain
by Amazon